Finding Justice in Perugia

a follow-up to Injustice in Perugia: a book detailing the wrongful conviction of Amanda Knox and Raffaele Sollecito

Bruce Fisher

FBI violent crimes investigator Steve Moore
www. InjusticeIn Perugia.org

Murder In Italy
Candace Dempsey

www. FriendsOfAmanda.org

To my beautiful wife and three amazing children for their
continued patience and unwavering support.

Contents

Preface

"Finding Justice in Perugia" is a follow-up to my first book *Injustice in Perugia* which showed in great detail that Amanda Knox and Raffaele Sollecito were both wrongfully convicted in December, 2009, for the murder of Meredith Kercher.

Amanda and Raffaele were trapped in a nightmare for 1427 days. During that time a movie was made, books were written, Wikipedia went haywire, online blog wars raged on, journalists were harassed, a rogue prosecutor remained on the job, an Anti-Knox hate group was formed, a grass roots effort became a force to reckon with, a retired FBI Agent raised eyebrows, even Italian politicians chimed in, all while Amanda and Raffaele sat in a prison cell never losing faith that their nightmare would eventually end.

"Finding Justice in Perugia" picks up where *Injustice in Perugia* left off, following the case throughout the appeal, detailing the side shows along the way, leading up to the day that Amanda and Raffaele finally found justice in Perugia.

Here is a brief summary of the case leading up the appeal for those who have not followed the case closely:

Who killed Meredith Kercher?

This was a horrific crime but not a complicated one. Unfortunately crimes of this nature are common throughout the world. Meredith Kercher was assaulted and brutally murdered by Rudy Guede when she walked into a burglary in progress in her own home. This case became complicated when authorities in Perugia, Italy, accused three innocent people of the crime, Amanda Knox, Raffaele Sollecito, and Patrick Lumumba.

The colossal error was fueled by Lead Prosecutor Giuliano Mignini who unfortunately did not look far for his suspects. Mignini immediately turned his focus to Amanda Knox and Raffaele Sollecito who were first to arrive at the crime scene. As Amanda and Raffaele watched the drama unfold, they did not realize that they too were being watched. Photos were taken showing the two embracing as they overlooked the cottage outside. It was a chilly day and Amanda was visibly cold, Raffaele tried to comfort her and at one point they shared a kiss. Amanda and Raffaele did not know it at the time, but at that moment, the world was closing in on them. Quick decisions were being made by investigators at the scene regarding the break-in, and members of the press were feverishly developing their opinions of the two based simply on a kiss.

Mignini's creative mind went to work creating a vision of how the crime took place. After observing the behavior of Amanda and Raffaele (a kiss), he imagined the crime started out as a sadistic sex game that turned into a brutal murder when Meredith refused to participate. His fantasy of a group sex game gone wrong was based on nothing more than his imagination. Elaborate visions were nothing new for Mignini. He already had a history of dreaming up satanic ritualistic murder fantasies. In Mignini's mind, the sadistic sex game he was referring to was instigated by a young woman who would lead the attack, ordering two men to force the victim to submit to sex, pushing the victim to her knees, torturing and killing her with one or more knives. Mignini dreamt up this story, wrote the script, and then began casting his characters.

Amanda Knox was cast as the lead. Amanda's boss, Patrick Lumumba, was cast in a supporting role and Raffaele Sollecito was cast as the boyfriend who was controlled by Amanda and would obey her orders. But something was wrong; Patrick had an airtight alibi. This was not surprising; after all, Mignini wasn't basing anything on evidence. He was simply looking to cast characters for his script.

The only evidence linking Patrick was a text message on Amanda's phone from Amanda to Patrick saying "See you later." This text was taken literally by the investigators but in the United States, this phrase, in the context that it was written, simply means goodbye. This phrase was either lost in translation or was intentionally twisted by the investigators to get the result they needed.

Investigators used this text message to pressure Amanda into implicating Patrick during an all night interrogation that I discussed in great detail in *Injustice in Perugia*. Amanda Knox was interrogated through the night of November 5 2007. Questioning was extremely aggressive, putting Amanda in a situation in which she had absolutely no control. She was thousands of miles from home in a country where she had a very limited knowledge of the language, being confronted by aggressive police officers who were accusing her of a horrible crime that she did not commit.

Amanda did not have a lawyer present during her interrogation; in fact she was told it would be worse for her if she did. Amanda was told that she was being questioned as a witness, but she was clearly being interrogated as a suspect. Italian law is very clear; no suspect is to be interrogated without the presence of an attorney. Therefore the interrogation of Amanda Knox was illegal.

Amanda testified in court that she was repeatedly slapped on the back of her head and called a stupid liar. The interrogator who slapped Amanda told her that she was trying to help her to remember. Amanda was also told they had proof that she was at the crime scene at the time of the murder. This was a lie. She was told that she was going to prison for 30 years and she would never see her family again.

Amanda was told that her boss Patrick Lumumba was the man that attacked Meredith. She did not give Patrick's name to the police; his name was suggested to her.

The interrogators attempted to connect Amanda to the crime by forcing her to imagine that she was at the cottage when Patrick committed the crime. None of it seemed possible to Amanda and she tried to explain to the police that nothing they were saying made any sense. She knew that she was not at the cottage at the time of the murder. She told the police repeatedly that she spent the night with Raffaele at his apartment and now they wanted her to imagine something completely different.

They kept telling her over and over again to imagine that she was at the cottage. When she still could not imagine what they were saying, she was slapped across the back of her head. Once again she was told to imagine that she was there but she could not do it. She knew what they were telling her was simply not true. The seemingly helpless situation left her feeling scared and confused. After many hours of interrogation, with nothing to eat or drink, exhaustion started kicking in. Amanda was trying to remember, she was trying to help—but what they were asking her to say just did not seem possible.

Then came another slap across the back of her head. You stupid liar! You were in the cottage! You will spend 30 years in prison! You are protecting a murderer! You will never see your family again!

Amanda was finally broken. She was desperate to end the questioning. She was extremely confused and she could not take any more abuse. After a long and grueling interrogation, twenty- year-old college student Amanda Knox gave in to her interrogators demands by describing an imaginary dream or vision. In this vision, she was in the kitchen covering her ears to block out screams while the man she worked for, Patrick Lumumba, was in Meredith's bedroom.

The police were kind enough to prepare the so-called confession for Amanda in their own words, as not one word in the typed out confession came from Amanda herself. At least twelve members of the police force interrogated Amanda. Why was it necessary for twelve people to interrogate a twenty-year-old female college student?

Later in the morning of November 6th, 2007, Amanda hand wrote a letter explaining the interrogation. Amanda wrote:

"In regards to this 'confession' that I made last night, I want to make it clear that I'm very doubtful of the verity of my statements because they were made under the pressures of stress, shock and extreme exhaustion."

Amanda was very confused and she was scared. This did not seem to matter to the police. As soon as they heard the information they wanted to hear, they went out and arrested Patrick Lumumba with no further questions asked.

Amanda's statements about Patrick were completely unreliable. Amanda tried to explain to the police that her statements were made during a time of stress, shock, and extreme exhaustion, and that she did not believe them to be true. After all, she was only repeating what the interrogators told her to say. At the time, the police simply did not care, and they arrested Patrick anyway.

Meanwhile, the police—unlike Mignini—were looking for actual evidence. Investigators found a handprint made in Meredith's blood on a pillowcase at the crime scene. The fingerprints pointed to an African male named Rudy Guede. Shortly after the murder, Rudy had fled to Germany. He was stopped in Germany trying to board a train without a ticket and was immediately extradited back to Italy. Mignini's storyline fell apart. Further investigation showed that all credible evidence at the crime scene pointed to Rudy Guede. His DNA was found on and inside Meredith's body. He also left his DNA on Meredith's purse. His DNA was also linked to feces left in the toilet. Though it was not known at the time, later discovery indicated that all of the shoeprints made in blood belonged to Rudy Guede.

The evidence was clear. There was no evidence at all to suggest that Meredith was killed during a satanic, ritualistic group sex game. Rudy Guede attacked and murdered Meredith Kercher—and he acted alone.

The actual facts did not matter to Mignini. Arturo De Felice, Perugia's police chief, and Edgardo Giobbi, the lead investigator from Rome, were already on board, and more importantly, Mignini had already told his fantasy to the press. The police held a press conference stating that they had evidence that all three killed Meredith because she refused to participate in a sex game. They boasted that the case was solid, boldly announcing, "Case closed."

How were they able to announce case closed before the evidence was analyzed? Edgardo Giobbi provided this explanation:

"We were able to establish guilt by closely observing

the suspects' psychological and behavioral reactions during the interrogations. We don't need to rely on other kinds of investigation as this method has enabled us to get to the guilty parties in a very quick time."

This decision of guilt was achieved before Giobbi had even heard of Rudy Guede. Giobbi also stated that his suspicions were raised just hours after the murder when he had seen Amanda at the crime scene swiveling her hips as she put on a pair of shoe covers. Amanda was considered guilty by the lead investigator before a single piece of evidence was even collected. Giobbi even hung a photo of Amanda Knox on his wall of Italy's most notorious criminals.

Mignini was already being investigated for abuse of office in relation to another case, so I have no doubt that he was desperate to protect his fragile reputation. It would be too embarrassing for those involved to admit their mistake and doing so could threaten their careers. Their initial theory had already achieved so much notoriety that any backtracking at that point would leave them looking foolish in the eyes of the world.

Mignini would see to it that evidence was collected to support his theory by cherry picking the pieces that could be made to fit and ignoring anything that would contradict. The actual break in was said to be staged, footprints having nothing to do with the crime were looked at as incriminating. Residual DNA, which is absolutely impossible to date, was said to be left on the night of the murder. All while real evidence such as blood patterns in the murder room showing the exact sequence of events to the trained eye was ignored, as was a possible fresh semen stain on Meredith's pillow that had been stepped in by Rudy Guede while still wet. All evidence suggesting one attacker was ignored.

On the night Meredith was killed we know from testimony that she spent the evening watching a movie and having a meal with friends. Meredith's friends said she commented that she was tired due to the Halloween parties from the night before and decided to call it an early evening. One of her friends walked her part way home shortly before 9 pm.

Meredith's mother was in the hospital at the time with a serious kidney disease and Meredith was in constant contact with her family to keep up to date with her mother's condition. The memory card in Meredith's cell phone shows that she tried to call her mother at 8:56 pm, on the evening of the murder, which would have been right around the time she arrived home. The call was never completed and there was no attempt by Meredith to call her mother back. If the call failed to go through, what kept Meredith from trying to call again?

The fact that Meredith made no further attempt to call her mother or contact anyone else to see why her call failed to go through suggests that she was attacked shortly after arriving home. She was also still wearing her jacket at the time of the attack.

At some point before Meredith arrived home for the evening, Guede entered the cottage through a bedroom, gaining entrance by breaking the window with a large rock. After entering the cottage, Guede needed to use the bathroom. His plans to burglarize the cottage were altered when Meredith arrived home for the evening. Meredith's arrival most likely surprised Guede. In his haste, he neglected to flush the toilet (leaving DNA evidence behind) as he made his way to Meredith's room. Guede surprised Meredith in her room, where he fatally stabbed and sexually assaulted her.

Expert analysis of the bloodstain patterns in the murder room shows the sequence of events that took place. The evidence shows that Guede attacked Meredith from behind and cut her throat. He removed Meredith's clothing when she was no longer able to fight back. He then moved Meredith out of the large puddle of blood so that he could sexually assault her in some manner. His DNA was found inside Meredith's body. He may have ejaculated on Meredith's pillow as there is an apparent semen stain at the scene. The court refused to have this stain tested as I will discuss in greater detail later in the book.

When Guede was finished in the murder room he went to the bathroom and cleaned himself up leaving streaks of Meredith's blood in the bidet and a bloody footprint on the bathmat. He then went back to Meredith's room and covered her body with a quilt from her bed. He sat on the edge of the bed placing the knife on the bed next to him, leaving a bloody imprint of the murder weapon on the bed sheet. He went through Meredith's purse taking her money, cell phones, and keys. He then walked out of her room, locking the door behind him leaving a trail of bloody shoe prints that ran down the hall toward the front door, becoming fainter with each step.

The evidence was clear, Rudy Guede ambushed Meredith Kercher in her own home, but with Mignini's reputation on the line, he sold a different story to the press for an entire year leading up to the first trial. Mignini leaked a series of lies to the media for the sole purpose of destroying the credibility of Amanda Knox, leaving Raffaele almost totally ignored. Amanda was the target of most of the leaks. Mignini successfully used the media to assassinate the character of Amanda Knox. Amanda never stood a chance. She was found guilty in the court of public opinion long before her trial ever began.

Judge Massei, the presiding judge in the first trial, saw to it that Mignini's hard work would pay off. Massei single handedly helped to secure the wrongful convictions by not allowing independent testing of the DNA evidence. Even though Massei did not buy Mignini's sex game theory he was more than willing to come up with a theory of his own.

Massei's theory of the attack is mind-boggling. Massei suggested that Amanda and Raffaele were being intimate in Amanda's room when they heard Meredith getting attacked by Guede. At that time, they both went to Meredith's room and witnessed the attack in progress. Influenced by smoking marijuana along with Raffaele's memories of violent comic books, they decided to join in on the attack. Massei's theory is not only ridiculous, his theory is insane. Why would Amanda decide to help a virtual stranger attack and murder her friend? Why would Raffaele just go along? How would they have known that Guede would not attack them? Are we really supposed to believe they both entered the room and saw the attack in progress, and not only had absolutely no fear of the attacker but also decided to assist in the attack?

Common sense told us that Amanda and Raffaele had absolutely nothing to do with Meredith's death but unfortunately common sense was nowhere to be found in Massei's courtroom. On December 4, 2009, on day 760 of their torturous nightmare, Amanda Knox and Raffaele Sollecito were wrongfully convicted. Amanda and Raffaele were left to hope that the court of appeals would see the truth or they would be faced with a quarter century behind bars for a crime they did not commit.

1

the fight for freedom – round two

On Wednesday, November 24, 2010 (day 1115), Judge Claudio Pratillo Hellmann swore in the jury of five women and one man, beginning the appeal trial for Amanda Knox and Raffaele Sollecito that would be expected to last as long as a year. As observed during the first trial, the Italian justice system moves very slowly. On appeal, Amanda and Raffaele, sentenced to 26 and 25 years respectively, would be given another chance to prove their innocence.

In Italy, the first appeal is essentially a brand new trial where evidence and testimony approved by the presiding judge is analyzed in the same fashion as the first trial. The standards are higher for jurors as they must all have a high school degree, unlike the first trial where the minimum required is only a middle school education.

Italy provides broad appeal rights to the accused granting two automatic appeals. If the first appeal fails, the case is then reviewed by the Italian Supreme Court to assure that there were no errors in procedure or application of the law. The second appeal does not re-examine the entire body of evidence.

The two appeal process has led to an overwhelming backlog of pending cases burdening the Italian justice system. This often causes overworked judges to rubberstamp previous judge's decisions, when pertaining to specific judgments made during trial, instead of taking the needed time to do a proper evaluation. Judges essentially clean off their desks knowing that the court of appeals will provide a safety net.

While Italy's appeal system might seem favorable to those convicted in the United States, many would stress the importance of getting it right the first time instead of relying on the appeals courts to clean up the mess. I do not intend to debate who has the better justice system, as the United States has an equal if not greater list of problems to contend with. But one thing is certain; if you are accused of a crime in Italy, you are likely to spend a great deal of time in prison fighting to prove your innocence.

Several conclusions can be reached on appeal in Italy; a complete acquittal, a conviction on lesser charge, or a reduction or increase in sentence. Prosecutors Mignini and Comodi appealed the first verdict, in hopes that the sentences would be increased to life, leaving much uncertainty to lie ahead for Amanda and Raffaele as the appeal got underway.

It needs to be noted that Rudy Guede, who already stands convicted of murdering Meredith Kercher, appealed his verdict and is now serving a reduced sentence of 16 years. Did anyone object to his reduction? Was there outrage that Guede was getting off easy? No, just complete silence. Mignini often voiced anger toward Amanda and Raffaele, usually in a vindictive tone that openly displayed his disgust for the two. Where was Mignini's anger for Rudy Guede? Why did Mignini harbor so much anger for Amanda and Raffaele without having similar feelings for Rudy Guede? You will see throughout this book that Rudy Guede has often been completely ignored or given a brief mention at the end of a conversation. You will see this in the media coverage, from bloggers, and even from Meredith's family. This alone is an unexplained tragedy.

Court hearings for Amanda and Raffaele would meet only once a week with lengthy delays throughout. The first few hearings would set the course of the trial. Even though the appeal offered a second chance and Judge Hellmann appeared to be well suited for the job, it was difficult for Amanda and Raffaele to be optimistic because justice had already failed them once. During the second appeal hearing on December 11, 2010 (day 1132), Amanda courageously stood up in court, making an emotional plea that left many in tears. Here is her statement translated into English:

"It used to happen a lot that some issue would be proposed for us to discuss amongst ourselves, debating our various opinions. I liked following these discussions, but I would get uncomfortable if I myself had to participate directly, because I'm not gifted in speaking. I often don't succeed in expressing my convictions, at least verbally, in the moment. In fact, among my friends, I'm the weakest at this. This is why one friend of mine often used to jokingly seize upon this notably more peaceful personality of mine, challenging me all the time by saying: "Stand up for yourself, Poindexter!" (This was a joke.)

Inevitably, I would respond, and my response would come out of my mouth incomprehensibly turned up around itself; either that, or I wouldn't manage to respond at all, because my mind would be blocked and my tongue tied. I wasn't able to do what my friend asked me to do, that is defend myself.

Imagine if I'm the weakest person in this courtroom at expressing myself. This is why I'm asking for patience, because what I have prepared are the things that I haven't succeeded in saying up to now. Or rather: I'm presenting myself to you for the second time; but these are the things I wish I had already said. I'm asking for your patience because there have been opportunities to speak before, and few words came out of me.

I admit that I often have a hard time finding the right words, because I never expected to find myself here: convicted of a crime I didn't commit. In these

4

three years, I have learned your language, and I have seen how your system works. But I've never gotten used to this broken life. I still don't know how to face all of this except by being myself -- which I have always been, notwithstanding the suffocating awkwardness. I was wrong to think that there are times and places to say important things; rather, important things just need to be said, and that's all.

The one thing I'm sorry about now is that there are people I want to speak to who aren't here. Still, I hope my words reach you, because either I'm locked up in prison or I'm here. And...I'm here.

To Meredith's family and loved ones, I want to say that I'm very sorry that Meredith isn't here anymore. I can't possibly know how you feel. But I, too, have little sisters; and the idea of their suffering, and of missing them infinitely, terrifies me. It is incomprehensible and unacceptable what you are experiencing, and what Meredith experienced.

I'm sorry that all this has happened to you, and that you will never have her with you, where she belongs. It's not right, and it can never be. But you are not alone as you remember her; I also remember Meredith, and my heart is broken for all of you. Meredith was kind, intelligent, friendly and always helpful. It was she who invited me to see Perugia with her, as a friend. I am grateful and honored to have been able to be in her company, to have been able to know her.

Patrick? I don't see you. But I'm sorry. I'm sorry because I didn't mean to do wrong to do you. I was very naive and not courageous at all; I should have been able to withstand the pressures that caused me to do harm to you. I didn't mean to contribute to what you have suffered. You know what it means to have unjust accusations imposed on your skin. You didn't deserve what you experienced and I hope you will be able to find peace.

Meredith's death was a terrible shock for me. She was a new friend, a reference point here in Perugia. And yet she was killed. Because I felt infinitely for her, I immediately recognized my own vulnerability in her death. I placed my trust especially in Raffaele, who proved to be a source of reassurance, consolation, helpfulness, and love. I also placed trust in the authorities who were conducting the investigation, because I wanted to help deliver justice for Meredith.

Another shock was to be arrested and accused. It took me a long time to confront the reality of being unjustly accused and redefined. I was in jail, and my face was everywhere. They were pouring onto me, almost always with insidious, unfair, awful gossip about my private life. Living this experience was unacceptable to me.

Above all, I placed trust in the hope that everything would be sorted out as it should have been; that this enormous mistake in my case would be recognized; and that every day I spent in my cell or in court was a day closer to the freedom that I was owed. This was my consolation in the darkness that allowed me to live without hope, doing my best to continue my life as I always have, in contact with my friends and loved ones, my family, dreaming of a future.

Now, I have been wrongfully convicted: more aware than ever of this experience and the harsh and undeserved reality. I still have hope for justice, and I still dream of a future -- even if this three-year experience is weighted with anxiety and fear.

Here I am, before you, more intimidated than ever. Not because I'm afraid or have ever been afraid of the truth, but because I have already seen the justice system fail me.

The truth about me and Raffaele has still not been recognized, and we are paying with our lives for a crime that we didn't commit. He and I deserve freedom, just like all the people in this courtroom today. We don't deserve the three years we have paid, and we certainly don't deserve any more. I am innocent; Raffaele is innocent. We didn't kill Meredith. I ask you to truly consider the possibility that there has been an enormous mistake in our case. No justice will be rendered for Meredith or her loved ones by making us pay for something we haven't done.

I am not the person the prosecution insists that I am -- at all. They would have you believe that I am a dangerous, diabolical, jealous, and violent girl who couldn't care less. Their theory depends on this. But I have never, ever been that girl. The people who know me are witnesses to the person I am. My past -- and I mean my real past, not the one told to you -- will show you that I have always been the way I really am. And if all this isn't enough, I ask you, I invite you, I ask you to ask the people who have been shaping me for three years. Ask them if I have ever been violent, aggressive, or uncaring faced with the sufferings that

*are part of the broken lives in prison -- because I
assure you that I am not like that.*

*I assure you that I have never resembled the
portrait painted by the prosecution. How is it possible
that I would be capable of jumping on such violence
as Meredith suffered? How is it possible that I would
have thrown myself like that at the opportunity to do
harm to a friend of mine? Seizing on such violence as
if it were more important and more natural than
everything I have been taught, all my values, all my
dreams, and all my life? None of this is possible. I am
not that girl. I am a girl who has proved to be what I
have always been.*

*I repeat that I too am asking for justice. Raffaele
and I are innocent and we deserve to live our lives in
freedom. We are not responsible for the death of
Meredith, and no justice is done, I repeat, by taking
away our lives from us. OK, thank you."*

At that moment, Amanda found her voice and her
heartfelt message was crystal clear. It would be up to
Judge Hellmann to correct the injustice committed
against Amanda and Raffaele. Whether he had the
courage to stand up to his peers was yet to be seen.

The appeals filed by both defense teams not only
requested a new trial but also detailed the evidence that
they wanted re-evaluated on appeal. It was Hellmann's
job to decide what items he would allow. During the third
hearing on December 18, 2010 (day 1139), Hellmann
made it clear what points he felt were crucial, adding that
other aspects of the case would be re-addressed in the
future if necessary.

Hellmann granted the defense request to put the prosecution's star witness, Antonio Curatolo, back on the stand and ordered the DNA evidence presented during the first trial to be analyzed by independent experts appointed by the court. The appeals filed by Amanda and Raffaele were built largely around a request for an independent review of forensic evidence so the fact that Hellmann was granting additional testing (refused by Judge Massei in the first trial) was great news for the defense. I truly believe that Amanda and Raffaele would have never been convicted in the first place if independent testing had been allowed during the first trial.

When Hellmann announced that the DNA would get a second look, Amanda could be seen taking deep breaths trying not to be overcome by her emotions, her mother and stepfather both began to cry and Raffaele beamed broadly at his family as if to say; finally someone is going to help us. Knowing they were innocent left the two with nothing to fear regarding additional testing. Their greatest fear was that the testing would never come.

Amanda's friend Madison Paxton, who moved to Perugia to support Amanda, said that she was "full of adrenaline" when Hellmann made the announcement. "This is an indication that they will look at this with fresh eyes" said Paxton.

At the time, it was disappointing to see that Hellmann did not include a possible semen stain on the list of evidence that would get a second look. This stain was found on Meredith's pillow in the murder room. Rudy Guede placed the pillow under Meredith's body during the attack. Forensics expert Francesco Vinci found this substance smeared in one of Guede's shoe prints on the pillow, proving the substance was wet at the time of the murder so it must have been deposited on the pillow at that time. Questions still remain as to why this substance was not tested during the first trial. Vinci had no doubt that the substance was semen but the court would not allow him to test it. Why? Investigators were presented with a murder with sexual assault and they neglected to test a substance that appeared to be semen. If the substance is semen and also belongs to Guede, it would further discredit the multiple attacker scenario as an assault of that nature does not fit into any theory ever established in court. Hellmann did not initially rule out future requests for additional testing, and he may very well have realized that the additional testing would have caused an unneeded delay to a trial that really hinged on two specific pieces of evidence.

Madison's observation that Hellmann would be looking at this case with a fresh pair of eyes appeared to be right on the mark, as Hellmann's course of action clearly showed that he was not influenced by the past but rather looking forward to the future. Hellmann's attention was directed right at the heart of the case. If the prosecution's star witness and the DNA evidence held up on appeal then Hellmann's court could easily confirm the convictions. If this crucial evidence was found to be unreliable, then the case against Amanda and Raffaele would be completely destroyed, all but guaranteeing their freedom. Openly expressing his views regarding his approach, Hellmann had this to say as the appeal was just getting underway:

> *"The only thing we know for certain in this complex case is that Meredith was murdered"*

During the fourth hearing on January 22, 2011 (day 1174), Hellmann appointed Stefano Conti and Carla Vecchiotti, from Rome's Sapienza University, to analyze the DNA. They would not complete their work until the end of June, giving the court plenty of time to fulfill Hellmann's request to re-examine the prosecution's star witness and take care of the twists and turns that would inevitably occur.

As expected, the appeal brought Amanda Knox back to the front pages, bringing more unwanted fame and a new series of sideshows. If dealing with the media was not stressful enough, Amanda's family and defense team would now be faced with fending off another attack on Amanda's character, but this time the culprit was not the news media.

2

the Lifetime debacle

Rumors of possible movie deals about Amanda Knox had been circulating for years but most believed a movie would come long after the court proceedings had concluded. So it was a surprise to many when the Lifetime network announced that they had a movie project in the works slated for early 2011 titled "Amanda Knox: Murder on Trial in Italy" starring Hayden Panettiere as Amanda Knox and Marcia Gay Harden as Amanda's mother Edda Mellas.

How can you write an accurate script without knowing the outcome of the trial? For the Lifetime network the answer to that question was simple; just say the movie is "based on a true story." Taking this route left little chance of a good outcome, not that Lifetime movies are held to a high standard, but any movie of this nature presented to the public with the trial still ongoing was dangerous and Lifetime executives should have known as much.

Thankfully Amanda's defense team was successful in getting the movie blocked in Italy so that perspective jurors would not be influenced. No matter what the outcome of the movie happened to be, it would be improper for any member of the jury to watch the film. Italy does not prevent jurors from interacting with the public or from obtaining information from the news and other forms of media which made it extremely important for Amanda's defense team to take action. At the time of this writing the lawsuit against Lifetime was still pending.

When the movie was announced, in a rare occurrence, all sides of the debate in this case agreed on something, as all believed that the movie was inappropriate. International outrage came quickly after Lifetime released trailers for the movie showing portrayals of Meredith Kercher being striped half naked in violent attack scenes. It was reported that Amanda Knox was sickened by the movie trailers when they flashed across her television screen in her jail cell. The defense teams for Amanda Knox, Raffaele Sollecito, Rudy Guede, and legal counsel representing the Kercher family, all objected to the film.

Unfortunately there was nothing to stop Lifetime from showing the movie to an American audience and the movie was aired for the first time in February 2011. The movie was wrought with inaccuracies and disrespectful to all involved. When Lifetime said "The Amanda Knox Story" was based on a true story, they were being disingenuous to their audience. This would be obvious to anyone that followed the case closely but could easily give the wrong impression to viewers who were hearing detailed information for the first time.

The director Robert Dornhelm took many liberties when making the movie. Hayden Panettiere's portrayal of Amanda Knox displayed demeanor throughout the film suggesting that that Amanda had something to hide. Facial expressions often speak louder than words on our television screens. While watching the movie I felt that Dornhelm was clearly attempting to put Amanda in a bad light.

One scene early on shows Amanda looking at Meredith with an angry tone that quickly turns into a smile when Meredith makes eye contact. There was never any witness testimony from anyone stating that Amanda ever showed any anger toward Meredith. The look seen on Amanda's face in that scene is the work of pure fiction.

A similar look can be seen on Amanda's face in an emotional scene when her mother has to tell her that she must remain in prison for over a year while police decide whether or not to charge her with the murder of her friend. We see Amanda sobbing as she goes to hug her mother and as soon as they embrace, we see a scary anger filled look on Amanda's face over her mother's shoulder.

Dornhelm goes to great lengths to imply that Amanda is fabricating her emotions and has something to hide.

Dornhelm's intentions are once again made clear in a scene showing Amanda alone in her prison cell, watching the news on television as Rudy Guede is indicted. An expression of deep worry is seen on Amanda's face as if she has a dark secret. The truth is that Amanda was grateful when Guede was indicted as she wanted whoever had brutally murdered her friend brought to justice.

Dornhelm adds dialogue to many situations where the characters were alone. Facial expressions and dialogue are key factors that influence viewers to form an opinion about the characters involved. Most viewers would not stop to think about that fact, instead taking the fictional dialogue as truth. We often see this with movies based on true stories as it is impossible to know exact dialogue, but this was a reckless path for Dornhelm to take given the fact that the actual real life trial was still ongoing.

Besides the general feel that Dornhelm was portraying to the audience based on the characters he envisioned, the movie is also filled with many factual errors. Some will seem less important than others but all work together to create the final product.

Amanda Knox and Meredith Kercher traveled to Italy to attend college. It is safe to say that one of the first things on their list would be to find a place to live. The movie suggests that Meredith found the room at the cottage before Amanda did when in reality Amanda signed the lease first. Is this a big deal? Not at all, but right from the start we see that Dornhelm does not feel the need to do basic research.

There are many small details that do not change the story line drastically but show carelessness on the part of the filmmakers. One scene shows Amanda's mother Edda Mellas at an airport in Perugia when she received the call from Amanda's stepfather Chris Mellas informing her that Amanda had been arrested. The truth is Edda was actually in an airport in Switzerland. Again, is this a big deal? Not at all, but some small details carry much more weight than others so it is important to make sure you have accurate facts for all details, no matter how big or small.

Take this small detail for instance; Amanda is shown working at a coffee shop before the murder took place, when a friend calls her Foxy Knoxy as if that was her current nick name at the time. This small detail is completely false, fueled by the real life Foxy Knoxy myth created by the media. Little details like this one can subtlety work to change the opinion of the viewer. Amanda was not called Foxy Knoxy by her friends.

There is an odd scene worth noting that shows Amanda and Raffaele skipping around in an open field having a picnic. Amanda and Raffaele had only known each other for six days and never had a picnic in the frigid month of October. I am not sure what Dornhelm was trying to suggest but the scene gave a clear sense that he had no real grasp of the actual story that he was recreating.

In another scene promoting pure fiction, we see Amanda and Raffaele looking immature at a candlelight vigil for Meredith, and then running away laughing and giggling. The truth is they were never there. Amanda and Raffaele did not attend the vigil. It needs to be noted that neither Meredith's British friends or her other roommates attended the vigil, so it was not unusual that Amanda and Raffaele were not there. The truth is that the two had been called back to the police station for more questioning that night and wanted to make sure they had something to eat beforehand. Why would Dornhelm take such liberties with this scene? Why would viewers be expected to believe this was fiction?

Dornhelm, once again showing that he did not care much for research, resurrected a long refuted myth about Raffaele in an attempt to show that Raffaele shared in the guilt that Dornhelm had wished on Amanda.

Amanda and Raffaele made the decision to call the police after they had discovered that the cottage may have been burglarized. The Postal Police were the first police to arrive at the cottage on November 2, 2007. They arrived to investigate two cell phones that were found in a nearby garden that were traced back to Amanda's housemate Filomena Romanelli. This visit was not out of the ordinary as the Postal Police handle this type of incident. The Carabinieri (the division of the police department that Raffaele called) arrived shortly after the Postal Police. The prosecution claimed that Amanda and Raffaele were surprised by the arrival of the Postal Police but the claim was proven to be complete nonsense. Raffaele stated that he had already phoned his sister and the Carabinieri before the Postal Police arrived. Raffaele's sister was a police officer at the time. Amanda and Raffaele were not surprised at all when the Postal Police showed up; in fact they assumed the Postal Police were the Carabinieri responding to Raffaele's call.

The prosecution claimed that Raffaele went and hid in Amanda's room and called the Carabinieri after the Postal Police arrived in order to make it look as if he and Amanda were not trying to avoid the discovery of the crime. This was simply not the case and fortunately for

Amanda and Raffaele there was proof to show what actually took place.

Video taken from a camera located in the parking garage across the street from the cottage supports Raffaele's claim. The clock on the garage camera was ten to twelve minutes slow. The prosecution completely misled and confused the public on this point by repeatedly stating the camera timer was fast.

The reason we know the clock is slow is because the camera shows a picture of a Carabinieri police car, and a Carabinieri officer with the distinctive stripe running down his trouser leg, in a clip time-stamped 1:22 pm on the day Meredith's body was discovered. However, at 1:22 pm, the Carabinieri were driving around, unable to find the place. They called Amanda's cell phone at 1:29 pm to ask for directions. Amanda handed the phone to Raffaele who handed it to one of the Postal Police, who explained how to get there. That call lasted four minutes and fifty seven seconds, meaning it did not end until 1:34 pm. Therefore, even if one assumes the call did not end until after the car appeared in the video, the clock had to have been at least ten to twelve minutes slow.

This is significant, because it means the camera footage shows the Postal Police arriving after Raffaele called the emergency number. The claim that he went and hid in Amanda's room, called his sister, and then called the emergency number twice, a series of calls that took about five minutes, is ludicrous. The details about Raffaele's calls were confirmed in court yet Lifetime chose to show the refuted lie in order to smear Raffaele. Why?

Dornhelm's scenes depicting the actual attack in no way give the viewer any sense of what actually occurred.

First, Meredith is shown striped down to her bra and panties when she is stabbed. In reality she was fully dressed when attacked because she had just arrived home. Rudy Guede's DNA was found on her jacket sleeve. Evidence shows that her jacket was violently pulled off of her body after it had already been soaked in blood. There is extensive proof showing that Meredith was not disrobed until after she was mortally wounded. Why would Dornhelm ignore these fundamental facts?

Second, the murder room shown in the movie was twice the size of the actual room. They even added a dresser! Ron Hendry did extensive research on this case for Injustice in Perugia and he showed in great detail that Meredith's bedroom was too small for the murder to have taken place as suggested by the prosecution. Four people struggling in a room of that size would have caused far more of a disturbance as Hendry describes here:

"Much of the room was undisturbed, including items on the desk, wall shelves, and the wall hangings. The nightstand may have been jostled, but several items were left untouched on it as well."

The brutal interrogation scene, in which the accusation of Patrick Lumumba was coerced out of Amanda was acceptable (if reviewed using made for TV standards), other than the fact that Amanda received no water. Unfortunately the movie leaves out an extremely important detail regarding what occurred shortly after the interrogation ended. During the interrogation Amanda signed 2 statements that were typed out for her (in Italian) by the police stating that she was in the kitchen of the cottage holding her ears as Meredith was being attacked in her bedroom by Amanda's boss, Patrick Lumumba. The film fails to mention that shortly after her interrogation ended, when Amanda was out of the high pressure situation, she wrote out a retraction. Here is an excerpt from her statement:

> *"In regards to this 'confession' that I made last night, I want to make it clear that I'm very doubtful of the verity of my statements because they were made under the pressures of stress, shock and extreme exhaustion."*

The film once again ignores Amanda's retraction when they show Mignini boldly shout out in anger that Amanda allowed an innocent man to languish in prison by not retracting her statement.

This brings us to the most egregious lie in the movie. On the day the murder was discovered, witnesses at the police station said they overheard Amanda discussing details of the crime scene. Amanda was in the kitchen of the cottage at the time so she did not see into the room when Meredith was discovered. Mignini's character charges in the film that Amanda could not have known those details on the first day, proving she participated in the crime.

The real life Mignini did make similar claims but they were refuted. The movie neglects to add that fact leaving viewers to believe that Amanda could not have possibly known the details she mentioned, therefore suggesting that she was guilty.

After the discovery of Meredith's body, everyone present at the cottage was ordered to the police station for questioning. Filomena, her friend Paola, and Paola's boyfriend Luca, had come to the cottage after Amanda and Filomena had exchanged several phone calls discussing the concern before the murder was discovered. Amanda and Raffaele would catch a ride to the police station in Luca's car. During the drive, Raffaele was discussing the details of the scene with Luca and Paola. Keep in mind, Amanda and Raffaele did not see into Meredith's room when the door was broken down, so Raffaele was looking for details from Luca and Paola because the two had looked into the room. Raffaele asked if Meredith was dead and if she had been murdered. Luca responded that Meredith was dead and that her throat had been cut. All of this talk proved to be too much for Amanda causing her to break down and cry. Paola testified in court that the conversation took place, completely refuting Mignini's claims. The court fully accepted the explanation for Amanda's knowledge, making Amanda's statements a non issue.

Why does Dornhelm go out of his way to suggest to viewers that Amanda had knowledge of the crime she could not have had unless she was involved? Furthermore, why did Dornhelm ignore known facts about the case purposely attempting to make Amanda look guilty? Why did Lifetime allow this garbage to be broadcast on their network? Hopefully these questions will eventually be answered in a court of law.

I have witnessed the damage done by this film firsthand, as several people have personally told me that they have concluded that Amanda is guilty, based on viewing the Lifetime movie. Even though I find it absolutely ridiculous that anyone would base their conclusions on a Lifetime project, there is no doubt that the movie had a negative effect on some of the viewers.

After the appeal reached a conclusion, Lifetime announced that it would revise the film before airing it again. If Lifetime had any integrity at all, the network would have apologized to its viewers for making the movie in the first place, announcing that the movie would never be aired again, followed by a personal apology to Amanda and Raffaele.

As the Lifetime disaster unfolded, it was disturbing to see Amanda attacked once again after already enduring several years of mistreatment by the media. Unfortunately Amanda was in a position where her character was being attacked from many different directions. Around the same time that her defense team was battling the Lifetime network, another battle was taking place online to correct another assault on Amanda's character.

3

The Wikipedia factor

I have to say that I had never given much thought about Wikipedia before I became involved with the Amanda Knox case. I would visit occasionally when searching for trivial information on Google, (as Wikipedia is usually at the top of most searches) and usually found Wikipedia useful when looking for information such as Betty White's age or wondering what actor played the principal in Ferris Bueller. I never wondered about the accuracy of the information on Wikipedia because, for what I was looking for, it was not really that important if it was wrong. I took an entirely different view of Wikipedia when I came to realize that many people were looking to the website for information regarding the Amanda Knox case.

Wikipedia is branded as an online free-content encyclopedia that anyone can edit and contribute to. This is true to an extent. Safeties are put into place by Wikipedia to insure that articles are not vandalized. These safeties can also prevent articles from being properly edited. Voluntary moderators are given permissions over time. When working together with other moderators, they can essentially take control of an article page blocking those who disagree with their point of view.

How do you gain permissions on Wikipedia? In order to work your way up the ladder on Wikipedia you need to be active on the site editing multiple pages in a variety of topics. This essentially means that editing articles on crochet, model airplanes, beanie babies, and many other wonderful hobbies will miraculously turn you into a credible Wikipedia editor giving you Wikipedia power. This structure is fine for hobbies and trivia; it fails miserably when it comes to articles of a serious nature such as the Amanda Knox case.

Why do I care about Wikipedia? I care because Wikipedia constantly finds itself at the top of Google searches, leading many to believe that it is accurate. I honestly do not know if this is based solely on popularity or if Wikipedia has an agreement with Google. No matter what led to their search engine success, one thing is clear; many people get their information from Wikipedia. This means that a Google search for "Amanda Knox" will put

Wikipedia's article front and center on the top of the page, making Wikipedia the first impression left on many who seek information about this case.

When I first read the Wikipedia article on this case in early 2010, I was very disappointed in what I found. The article misrepresented evidence, gave false information of the accused, misrepresented the prosecutor, omitted incriminating information about Meredith's killer Rudy Guede, provided misleading information about the support that Amanda received, and contained various other fabricated claims.

When I began my research I discovered that the problem with Wikipedia was twofold. First, Wikipedia did not allow a page dedicated to Amanda Knox and Raffaele Sollecito. Second, the page dedicated to Meredith Kercher was loaded with incorrect information sourced mainly from British tabloids and was being guarded by a small group of stubborn editors that had earned their Wiki powers. Further research showed that this small group not only controlled the article but had deleted the entire original article and replaced it with an entirely new version of their own.

The only Wikipedia page allowed on this topic at the time was titled "Murder of Meredith Kercher." Of course, I have no objection to a page dedicated to Meredith Kercher. Meredith should forever remain the focus of the initial crime; but the trial of Amanda Knox and Raffaele Sollecito has been extremely controversial with many feeling early on that Amanda and Raffaele were wrongfully accused. Wikipedia does not provide pages for every murder that occurs on earth, as that would be an impossible task. Wikipedia's policies allow "notable" murders to be discussed. It is important to look at why Meredith's murder was considered notable.

Meredith's murder became worldwide news due to the lurid details that were reported early on. These details, that proved irresistible for the media, came from descriptions of those accused of the crime. If Rudy Guede had been arrested early on as he should have been, the crime would have not been discussed on a grand scale. It would have been just one of the many other unfortunate murders that occurred in the world. A woman was murdered during a burglary. This crime was gruesome but not complicated. The lurid details were all a fantasy resulting in the wrongful conviction of Amanda Knox and Raffaele Sollecito.

Unfortunately, Wikipedia only allowed minimal discussion of the obvious controversy, completely ignoring the fact that Amanda and Raffaele were the notable story. Any attempts to edit the Meredith Kercher article to include these details was forbidden and considered "off topic." Keep in mind this is the only page made available on Wikipedia to discuss the entire case. Even though this case has been called "the trial of the century" and hundreds of articles have been written discussing the controversy, Wikipedia refused to acknowledge it. How can Wikipedia be called an encyclopedia when they pick and choose what events in history they will permit discussion of?

Why does Wikipedia allow censorship of information? Further research showed me that this was happening for a couple of reasons. First, the editors controlling the page thought Amanda and Raffaele were guilty. Second, Wikipedia's source guidelines allowed those biased editors to maintain control. Wikipedia relies on news outlets as their main source of information for articles of this nature. If the news gets it wrong then so does Wikipedia.

Wikipedia is not properly designed to handle articles like the Meredith Kercher article. What makes Wikipedia so dangerous is the fact that it's most often correct, leading people to believe that it is a credible source of information for all topics. Being correct a majority of the time is fine if you are reading about the Batmobile but completely unacceptable when reading about an ongoing murder trial. When it comes to the Meredith Kercher article, Wikipedia was not acting as an encyclopedia. It has been more like a controlled media guide.

Many people like me signed up to Wikipedia to try and improve the article. My contribution was very small but I observed the Meredith Kercher article closely as new users attempted to join the discussion. Unfortunately it did not go smoothly, as all new users were instantly labeled as "newbies" or "single purpose accounts," and not looked at fondly by those in control. It took me a while to come to terms with the fact that users with names like SuperMarioMan were controlling the information being provided. The truth was that most of the editors that were holding the Meredith Kercher article hostage spent most of their time editing comic book pages and various science fiction topics (as could be seen by looking at their edit histories). Somehow Wikipedia felt that this group was best suited to edit articles about serious murder cases.

Wikipedia is not fond of experts or expert opinion. In fact they tend to frown on experts that wish to participate. If you invented the toaster, Wikipedia does not want you writing the article on the toaster, they would prefer that a group of college students Google everything they can find about the toaster and create the article with no input from you.

Wikipedia policies made it very difficult to gain any ground on correcting the inaccuracies of the Meredith Kercher page. News articles were the only sources we were able to work with, and anyone that followed the case from the beginning knows that the media did a horrible disservice to the public with their inaccurate coverage.

If finding accurate sources was not challenging enough, new users were also finding themselves under constant attack from veteran Wikipedia users. At one point in one drastic sweep, many new users were banned from Wikipedia being accused of "meatpuppetry." This term refers to contributions made by new Wikipedia members that are suspected of having been recruited by an existing member to support a certain position. Others were accused of being "sockpuppets." This term refers to a banned user coming back using a fake name. I was accused of being a sockpuppet for no reason whatsoever. I was investigated by a small group of Wiki veterans that simply wanted to irritate me and cause me to disappear. I did not mind because I knew I was not a sockpuppet, in fact I signed up using my real name.

The lame attempt to have me removed from Wikipedia failed but I still remain on a hit list created by a user named Pablo that was designed to keep track of single purpose accounts. Of course Pablo objected to me calling it a hit list and said we were not being targeted. I still find his logic baffling. What else could a list of that nature possibly be used for?

One victim of the massive meatpuppet sweep was Jim Lovering (Charlie Wilkes). Jim had made just one edit when he was swept into the group and banned. Jim has vast knowledge of this case and also has access to the case files. He would have been more than happy to provide court documents, photographs, and video to help improve the article. Many other quality editors were eliminated in the same fashion assuring that the article remained biased and inaccurate.

Correcting the problems with the Wikipedia article seemed hopeless but one man would not give up the fight long after many of us had considered it a lost battle. That man is Joseph Bishop. In March 2011, Joseph wrote an open letter to Wikipedia Founder Jimbo Wales asking that he and others in positions of influence at Wikipedia take a careful look at Wikipedia's coverage of the Meredith Kercher murder.

Here is Joseph Bishop's petition to Wikipedia founder Jimbo Wales:

Dear Mr. Wales:

We are a group of citizens concerned with the fairness of the recent trial of Amanda Knox and Raffaele Sollecito. We ask that you and others in positions of influence at Wikipedia take a careful look at Wikipedia's coverage of the subject. The Murder of Meredith Kercher article in its present form is not written from a neutral point of view and bears little resemblance to what reliable sources have said about the case.

The trial of Amanda Knox and Raffaele Sollecito has emerged as one of the most controversial and heavily criticized judicial proceedings in modern European history. None of this is properly reflected in the Wikipedia article which for the most part relies on obsolete and inaccurate British tabloid reports for its information. The omission from the article of the criticism of the numerous important experts who have stated in no uncertain terms that Knox and Sollecito did not receive a fair trial calls into question the article's neutrality. Other flaws in the article include false statements about luminol evidence, the de-emphasis of Rudy Guede and Giuliano Mignini's criminal acts prior to the crime, and the characterization of the support for Ms. Knox as a PR campaign. Until recently, the article contained a fabricated claim that the Rudy Guede's apartment had been purchased for him by a wealthy Perugian family.

The article goes on to seriously misrepresent the statements made by Knox and Sollecito during interrogation. In fact both had repeatedly given the true version of events that they were at Sollecito's apartment together and only toward the end after hours of intense pressure did Ms. Knox make any statements about Patrick Lumumba which were later shown to be false.

The reliable sources who have criticized the trial include John Q. Kelly, Judy Bachrach, Douglas Preston, Paul Ciolino, Timothy Egan, Peter Van Sant, Steve Moore, Bob Graham, Michael Scadron, Judge Michael Heavey, George Fletcher, Dr. David Anderson, and US Senator Maria Cantwell. These people have spoken in important media such as CNN, CBS, ABC, The Independent, and the New York Times and they have all used unprecedented language to condemn the trial. On Larry King Live two separate commentators described the tribunal as a "public lynching" and a "kangaroo court." New York Times columnist Timothy Egan compared it to the Salem Witch Trials. In a CBS News segment, long time correspondent Peter Van Sant stated, "We have concluded that Amanda Knox is being railroaded."

The current, mostly European, Wikipedia moderators who have taken ownership of the article are determined to see that this criticism is not presented to the readers. In addition, the article's list of books and television documentaries about the case deliberately omits certain works that conflict with the agenda of the article's moderators.

Wikipedia has a reasonably well conceived set of guidelines regarding biographies of living persons (which include Amanda Knox and Raffaele Sollecito) but they have not been properly applied to this article. Clear and compelling documentation of irregularities in the article and in the conduct of the article's moderators have been presented to Wikipedia without a proper response.

Wikipedia content is supposed to be based on what reliable sources have said about the subject, yet the current article has now been explicitly condemned by the authors of two different books about the case. As an example, Dr. Mark Waterbury, author of Monster of Perugia, writes, "the Wikipedia entry for the Meredith Kercher case has been corrupted by partisan activity, and as of this writing, it is deliberately biased and inaccurate."

While mainstream media coverage has been increasingly favorable to Ms. Knox, it has been offset to some degree by a formidable online campaign of what can only be described as "hate speech" by those who see her as guilty. It is members of this camp who have hijacked the Wikipedia article. At this point, powerful Wikipedia moderators with a non-neutral agenda have successfully blocked or threatened away a dozen editors who have challenged the neutrality of the present article. We know of no other article where the integrity of Wikipedia has been compromised to this degree.

Please do something about this Mr. Wales. All we are seeking is an article that accurately reflects what reliable sources have said about the case.

Sincerely, the Undersigned

Mr. Wales read the letter and decided it warranted his attention. Here's what he had to say:

"This blog post likely deserves some attention. My interest is simply in making sure that this entry accurately reflects what reliable sources have said and that no reliable sources are omitted based on anyone's agenda in either direction. I'm posting this notice on the BLP noticeboard and the talk page of the article."

You would think that veteran Wikipedia editors would be honored that Wikipedia's founder stopped by to take a look at an article they were working on, but amazingly that was not the case.

Here are some of the warm welcomes Mr. Wales
received:

> *"An internet petition with all of 60 signatures? Hmm,
> I am not seeing the compelling need for the founder to
> get involved here."*

> *"I think you really needed to spend more time
> researching before wading into this debate."*

> *"Sorry, but exactly which objections require real
> answers?"*

The group of veteran editors that hijacked the Meredith
Kercher article was ready and waiting when Mr. Wales
joined the discussion. Thankfully Mr. Wales had the
patience to deal with his unwelcome arrival. Here are
some of his responses:

> *"A petition doesn't matter. Number of signatures
> doesn't matter. Getting it right is all that matters. I
> accept input from all kinds of sources, and we should
> always be willing to take another look."*

> *"I consider it our greatest honorable trait that we are
> always willing to take another look, always willing to
> review our work, and always willing to accept
> criticism. The post raises several quite
> straightforward objections that deserve to be
> answered with real answers, not jeers."*

When hostility continued throughout the discussion, Mr. Wales had this to say:

"You might find it more pleasing to drop the hostility and actually listen to what I am saying."
"I am concerned that since I raised the issue, even I have been attacked as being something like a "conspiracy theorist". I would like to bring this issue to the attention of the wider community, and I continue to do my own research."

"I am doing my own research, and it doesn't look good. I see editors being blocked for single edits that are absolutely defensible on the thinnest of grounds. That's not acceptable."

"Whenever we see outrage in the face of mere questions, it is good to wonder where the truth lies."

Injustice in Perugia was very pleased to see Jimbo Wales taking an interest in the case. His presence allowed editors to participate in the discussion and work out proper consensus in order to get edits of the article approved. It would have been ideal if Jimbo would have agreed that Wikipedia was not the proper format for articles about ongoing murder cases but that would be wishful thinking. I understand that Jimbo would shy away from discouraging any type of traffic coming to Wikipedia.

Jimbo was very professional in how he handled his involvement with this subject. Thankfully he was not swayed by disparaging comments, but he was limited, as were we, by his own website's guidelines. I am hopeful that this case will cause Jimbo to re-evaluate certain aspects of his website. Wikipedia is an enormous success which in turn brings enormous responsibility.

The Wikipedia article discussing the Meredith Kercher murder case along with the wrongful conviction case of Amanda Knox and Raffaele Sollecito never had a chance of being fully corrected until the trial had ended. Only then would the media finally provide the necessary sources needed to create an accurate Wikipedia article on the case.

At the time of this writing, those who have long held the article hostage are losing their grip as their cherished media sources slowly but surely evaporate. In a positive move forward, a new article has now been allowed for Amanda Knox and a separate article discussing the trial of Amanda and Raffaele has also been created. Yes, time will eventually correct the article that has been an embarrassment to Wikipedia for years, but when that time comes it will be far too late to correct the damage that it has caused.

During a discussion on Wikipedia as positive changes were being implemented, one user asked me why I was still discussing the past article; changes were being made, so all was well. I was told once again that the article of the past conformed to Wikipedia's guidelines, and now with the new information provided by the outcome of the trial, the revised article would do the same. The errors of the past were easily explained away because the original article met Wikipedia's guidelines.

I am amazed that many of the Wiki veterans are so hung up on Wikipedia policy that they have lost the ability to use common sense, essentially becoming Wiki robots. Wikipedia misrepresented this case to the public for nearly four years, and now, like many others,

Wikipedia owes Amanda and Raffaele an apology. The problem is that too many Wiki veterans will never come to realize what they have done, because when thinking in terms of Wikipedia, they appear to have lost the ability to think as human beings.

I would suggest for those involved with Wikipedia to refrain from rejoicing that the case is finally being reported correctly, and to instead use this as a learning experience. It is crystal clear that Wikipedia is the wrong format for cases like this. Wikipedia should learn from their mistakes and work to make proper changes to prevent this from happening again.

Wikipedia also needs to do a better job of highlighting its limitations to its readers. It is important to realize what Wikipedia is only as reliable as the editors that control it. Wikipedia addresses the question of reliability on their website if you know where to look. Here is what Wikipedia has to say:

"The reliability of Wikipedia articles is limited by the external sources on which they are supposed to rely, as well as by the ability of Wikipedia's editors to understand those sources correctly and their willingness to use them properly. Therefore, articles may or may not be reliable, and readers should always use their own judgment. Students should never use information in Wikipedia (or any other online encyclopedia) for formal purposes (such as school essays) until they have verified and evaluated the information based on external sources. For this reason, Wikipedia, like any encyclopedia, is a great starting place for research but not always a great ending place."

Wikipedia's explanation leaves an important question unanswered; who is responsible for telling the public that the website consistently finding itself at the top of web searches for any given topic is not intended to be seen as reliable? You would certainly never know Wikipedia's position by viewing their home page.

Is it Wikipedia's fault that most readers stop by to gather information without researching the truth about Wikipedia? I suppose an argument can be made either way. Maybe the more important question to ask is whether or not Wikipedia is misleading the public by calling their website an encyclopedia.

4

a witness demolished

On March 26, 2011 (day1237), the prosecution's star witness, Antonio Curatolo, would once again find himself under the spotlight, and this time the defense was eager to shine the light a little brighter. Curatolo was the only supposedly credible eye witness brought forward by the prosecution during the first trial. He is the only person that claimed to have seen Amanda and Raffaele near the crime scene shortly before the murder.

Curatolo was a homeless man (he now has a home in prison) that admitted to using heroin on a daily basis and admitted that he was on heroin the night he claimed to have seen Amanda and Raffaele. Curatolo's question and answer session on appeal left many wondering how his testimony could have possibly helped to secure the conviction of Amanda and Raffaele in the first trial.

In 2009, Curatolo testified that he had seen Amanda and Raffaele in Piazza Grimana, a square overlooking the cottage, on the night of the murder. His testimony completely backfired when at one point he actually provided an alibi for Amanda and Raffaele. Judge Massei was determined to make Curatolo's testimony work, leading him to disregard a large portion of his testimony in the court's motivation report. Massei cherry picked what he needed in an attempt to claim that Curatolo stated he saw Amanda and Raffaele before the murder took place.

Curatolo testified nine times that he saw Amanda and Raffaele hanging around outside from 11:30 pm to 12:00 am. This testimony contradicted the prosecution's suggested time of attack actually providing an alibi for the two if you were to believe the prosecution's time line. Curatolo testified only once that he saw Amanda and Raffaele around 11:00 pm. Massei ignored nine statements made by Curatolo and chose to believe the one statement that he needed to support the court's decision. Nine out of ten times, Curatolo said the exact same thing. One time he altered his statement, and that one slip was good enough for Massei.

A kiosk vendor who was doing business near Curatolo's bench contradicted his testimony, highlighting how easily Curatolo became confused about each day's events. The woman had set up her kiosk near Curatolo's bench on the day in question. She stated she saw Curatolo on the morning of November 2 on the bench at 6:40 am when she opened her kiosk. Curatolo claimed that he slept in the park and did not get up till 8:30 or 9:00 am.

Curatolo was also confused about what day he was referring to. He claimed that on the evening he saw Amanda and Raffaele, he left the piazza after he saw several buses full of young people leaving for the discos. However, there were no disco buses running that night because all of the discos were closed. This observation, along with the kiosk owner's testimony, clearly shows that Curatolo was most likely remembering a different night.

Of course, the court decided to accept Curatolo's testimony. Well, sort of. They accepted the part they liked, and decided to simply ignore the fact that Curatolo provided an alibi for Amanda and Raffaele in nine of his ten statements.

The appeals court was not so welcoming to Curatolo and his brief time on the stand did not go smoothly for him. Curatolo's question and answer session with the court's second Judge Massimo Zanetti went as follows:

> Judge: So, you saw Amanda and Raffaele?
> Curatolo: Yeah, it was Halloween when I saw them. I know this because I saw the kids getting on the disco buses all dressed up in costumes. That's how I also know what time it was.
> Judge: When is Halloween?

Curatolo: I don't know. Maybe end of October or beginning of November, I think.

Judge: You aren't sure? What about your case now? You are in prison, correct? How long will you be there?

Curatolo: I don't know. I don't understand the case against me really. I understand nothing.

Judge: Ok, so how did you live in the park? Were you always there?

Curatolo: Always, yes. I never left. I just lived there. On a bench mostly.

Judge: What about when you had to go to the restroom?

Curatolo: I went to the bathroom in the wooded area down the hill.

Judge: So you weren't there all the time then?

Curatolo: What do you mean?

Judge: Never mind. So, are you certain the buses were disco buses and not tour buses?

Curatolo: Yes, definitely disco buses. They look different from other buses.

Prosecution: No, no, you must be mistaken?

Curatolo: No. I am certain they were disco buses.

Judge: Do you take drugs?

Curatolo: Yes, heroin.

Judge: Were you taking drugs on that night?

Curatolo: I always take drugs, so most certainly I was high that night…but that's ok. Heroin does not make you hallucinate or anything.

Judge: Guards, take him away. I am done.

Curatolo's testimony confirmed what the defense had been saying for years; Curatolo was not a reliable witness. The defense further proved this one hearing prior to Curatolo's appearance when they called bus drivers to testify that no disco buses were running on the night in question. Judge Zanetti's visible disgust with Curatolo was evidence enough to show that his testimony would not be accepted by the appeals court. The prosecution's star witness was officially demolished on appeal.

As discussed in chapter one, Judge Hellmann's priorities were to look at the prosecution's star witness and the DNA evidence. The first order of business was complete and it was a sound victory for the defense. It was no time to celebrate but it was good to see the appeal moving in the right direction.

As the years passed, Amanda found the strength to speak out about her innocence. This tragedy forced her to grow up fast and robbed her of vital years of her young life. At the end of the March 26 hearing, Amanda courageously stood up in court once again making an emotional well composed statement:

> "I have been in prison for three years now and I am innocent. It is very frustrating and it is mentally exhausting and I want the truth to be found," she said, speaking in Italian, "There have been many mistakes and many prejudices"

Tearing up, Amanda went on to say:

> "I remember how I was young and how I did not understand anything and the most important thing is that I do not want to stay in prison unjustly for all my life"

Amanda's words were those of an innocent person. She wanted the truth to be found. Amanda wanted the DNA evidence analyzed again knowing that her and Raffaele had absolutely nothing to do with Meredith's death. The last thing a guilty person wants is for their DNA to be looked at more closely. Time was needed for the independent experts to complete their DNA analysis so the next hearing was not scheduled until May 21, 2011. Once again, all Amanda and Raffaele could do was wait.

As it turned out the debate over the DNA evidence would have to wait even longer than expected because the independent experts requested a 40-day extension to complete their work. Hellmann granted their request, ruling that the final report must be submitted to the court by June 30 so that it could be discussed at a hearing in July.

This delay guaranteed that the trial would extend beyond the summer recess into the fall, meaning that Amanda and Raffaele would endure another scorching hot summer in prison. Even though both were disappointed by the delay, they both expressed the importance of the task at hand. Their freedom relied on the DNA tests being conducted properly so if more time was needed then it would be well worth the wait.

5

the architects of the Foxy Knoxy myth

With the appeal in full swing, the public had now seen the prosecution's only eye witness fully discredited. That information along with confirmation that the DNA was finally being analyzed by court appointed experts no doubt influenced public opinion to continue to shift strongly in the favor of innocence and many journalists were now taking note.

Media coverage of this case definitely played a role in the wrongful conviction of Amanda Knox and Raffaele Sollecito. Amanda was mistreated horribly by the media with disparaging headlines that were endless. With the help of the media, prosecutor Giuliano Mignini's fictional character, the satanic ritualistic sex crazed killer, Foxy Knoxy was born. As we would all later find out, Foxy Knoxy was not a sex crazed killer after all. She was a sweet innocent eight year old soccer player. Amanda Knox was given the nickname as a child for her sly moves on the soccer field. By the time the world found out who the real Foxy Knoxy was, it was too late. The damage was done.

While the common wisdom is that the tabloid media played a major role in spreading lies and misinformation, the reality is that these disparaging headlines and salacious articles were not confined simply to common tabloids, but to well known magazines as well, such as *Newsweek*.

A trio of yellow journalists have been the worst offenders. These journalists are Nick Pisa, Barbie Nadeau and Andrea Vogt. These three journalists were the chief architects of the Foxy Knoxy myth and have fueled the Anti-Knox fervor working as mouthpieces for Giuliano Mignini, the corrupt and convicted prosecutor that secured the convictions against Amanda and Raffaele.

Nick Pisa, a freelance journalist from the United Kingdom who writes often for The Daily Mail, has recently shifted his opinion on the case, now leaning toward innocence. Regrettably however, his change of heart is too little too late because of the damage he has already caused. In fact, he was the first reporter to use the name "Foxy Knoxy" after browsing Amanda's MySpace page looking for dirt. The catchy nick-name was very attractive to the media helping to fuel Mignini's myth.

Pisa's tabloid sensibilities were loud and clear shortly after an appeal hearing in September when Amanda appeared to bow her head momentarily in court. This prompted Pisa to contact the family, looking to see if Amanda had "passed out." As it turned out Amanda was completely fine leaving Pisa without his shocking headline.

Barbie Nadeau, who reports for the Daily Beast, did not disappoint her fans with her rapid fire tweeting from the pressroom during the appeal hearings. In fact she earned the award for most tasteless tweet for this gem: "Court discussing the appropriate way to cut a bra off a dead body. Where is a mannequin when you need one?"

Nadeau exhibited an obvious bitterness during the appeal; a resentment that most likely stems from being on the wrong side of history. Nadeau, who published a book after the first trial under the title: "Angel Face: The True Story of Student Killer Amanda Knox" must have felt awkward after the appeal, eventually changing the title of her book to: "Angel Face: Sex, Murder and the Inside Story of Amanda Knox." At one point, Nadeau hilariously tweeted that she was actually objective, somehow forgetting the ill-conceived title of her book.

During the appeal, Nadeau wrote an article for the Daily Beast suggesting that Meredith Kercher's actual killer might receive a get out of jail free card if Amanda and Raffaele were allowed to walk. To anyone who understands the forensics in this case, this line of thinking is beyond absurd, as all credible evidence in this case points directly at Rudy Guede. Unfortunately, Nadeau had little choice but to go pursue the "Amanda got away with it" angle. Whether she likes it or not, Nadeau is one of the main faces of the yellow journalists who forced Amanda's guilt down her readers' throats, all while distorting facts, using sloppy analysis and in some cases stating outright lies.

During the appeal, bestselling author Douglas Preston who wrote *the Monster of Florence*, confirmed Nadeau's feelings for Amanda and her family when he revealed that Nadeau openly admitted that she despises Amanda's family and she called the Friends of Amanda support group a "cult." Nadeau made these comments approximately three years ago, yet she continues to present herself as an objective journalist with regard to this case.

Andrea Vogt, who has written freelance pieces for Seattlepi.com, attended much of the first trial. Although absent during most of the appeal, it did not keep her from continuing to spread lies about the case.

Vogt wrote an article in February 2011 titled *"Italian judges' report: Amanda Knox says she 'was there'"* that misrepresented a statement made by Amanda Knox during the initial investigation. Amanda was heard telling her parents "I was there" during a taped conversation in prison. Amanda was telling her mother she was at Raffaele's apartment. Amanda was not talking about the crime scene. When questioned in court about this statement, Amanda's explanation was accepted by the court and never brought up again. Vogt was in court on the day of the testimony, yet she still reported that the statement suggested that Amanda was at the crime scene.

This amazing omission can only be attributed to total ineptness or actual malice.

Why would any credible journalist willingly report misinformation? In another article titled "Knox is no Innocent," Vogt judges Amanda's character based on her doodles and eyebrow movements. Amazingly, she was able to remember those fine details during her court visits but somehow forgot about Amanda's testimony discussing the "I was there" comment. It is unlikely Vogt had a simple mental lapse and this omission was obviously intentional.

Toward the end of the appeal, Vogt began working on a documentary about Amanda Knox that was expected to air sometime after the verdict. In an amazing and ridiculous course of events, she actually sent an email to Amanda's family saying that they had her permission to ask to be in her documentary. Yes, you read that correctly. The family of Amanda Knox was told they could ask to be in Andrea Vogt's presumably horrible documentary which is about their own daughter! Keep these things in mind when you hear certain journalists talk about how objective they are.

Vogt has had an intimate relationship with Anti-Knox bloggers since as early as 2008, interviewing them as objective sources without disclosing that they had been blogging under fake names about their belief in Amanda's guilt long before she ever even had a trial.

Vogt's propensity for quoting Anti-Knox bloggers as legitimate sources had not been confined to isolated incidents. Rather, she has kept up this pattern consistently for years. Very early in the case, Vogt quoted a woman named "Laura Wray" under the guise that she was an objective source, when in fact she had been blogging on

Amanda Knox hate sites as early as 2008. Additionally, Laura Wray only possesses a Bachelor's Degree in science and was not qualified to answer Vogt's questions.

However, "Laura Wray" was not the first Anti-Knox blogger Vogt would quote as an objective source. In January 2009, before Amanda had even been tried for murder, Vogt wrote an article for the Italian publication *Panorama* in an article entitled *"Meredith's Murder Divides Seattle."* In the article she quoted a man named Randy Jackson, who is now the co-moderator of the Anti-Knox site Perugia Murder File (more to come regarding this group in chapter nine). Vogt quoted Jackson as if he was an objective source without revealing that he had been blogging about his belief in Amanda's guilt for some time. That same article quoted a woman named Kris Arneson who had also been blogging on Amanda Knox hate sites quite frequently. Again, this fact was not revealed. One would assume an objective journalist would give some sort of disclosure in all these instances, but Andrea Vogt never did any such thing. Her consistent interviewing of Amanda Knox hate bloggers raises serious questions about her honesty and closeness to these sites.

The architects of the Foxy Knoxy myth, (Andrea Vogt, Barbie Nadeau and Nick Pisa) were interviewed together, in September 2011, along with an Italian television producer, Sabina Castelfranco, for Dateline Australia. Pisa appeared blatantly uncomfortable throughout the video as Vogt and Nadeau spoke of well-known falsehoods as if they were common facts; the largest being that there was mixed blood found at the crime scene (100% not true). To Pisa's credit, he managed to interject a little common sense when he said that the case would have never gone to trial in the United Kingdom due to a lack of evidence.

However, Pisa threw journalistic ethics out the window when he pathetically attempted to explain away his horrendous reporting on this case by placing the sole blame on the authorities in Perugia, espousing the principle that you should just write what the police tell you:

> *"If you're getting some information from a primary source - like a police officer, like a prosecutor - you've got to take it at face value, you've got to believe what you're being told"*

Of course this logic is beyond ridiculous. If this were a journalistic standard to strive for, we would not need journalists in crime cases—rather we could just have the police write the articles themselves.

In the jaw dropping interview, Vogt and Nadeau continued to promote the egregious lie that there was mixed blood at the crime scene. Both frequently repeat that Meredith's blood was mixed with Amanda's blood in several different places in the cottage. Mixed blood was never claimed by the prosecution, and no testimony was heard at trial. But Nadeau, being the advanced forensic scholar that she is would not let facts get in the way, giving case followers this analogy:

> *"I live in a house with three people (my two sons and my husband); I guarantee you I have never mixed blood with any of them anywhere in the house; I don't bleed where they bleed; we never bleed at the same time."*

Yes, she actually said this in the interview. Whenever you read something this ridiculous, it is no wonder the media has gotten this case so wrong. With utterances like these, we are not exactly dealing with sophisticated minds amongst the guilt purporting journalists in this case.

The truth is Meredith's blood mixed with residual DNA that was already present in the cottage long before the murder took place. Amanda was examined by the police and no wounds were found on her body. Amanda was not bleeding, but more importantly, she was not there. Amanda's blood never mixed with Meredith's blood anywhere at any time.

After nearly four years, if the architects of the Foxy Knoxy myth still cannot understand simple falsehoods like these, is it any wonder why the public has been so misinformed in this case? Readers deserve better than the tabloid principles of Nick Pisa, the illogical musings of Barbie Nadeau and the terribly sourced articles of Andrea Vogt.

Another reporter that must be called out for his reprehensible coverage of this case is John Follain. I neglected to mention Follain in "Injustice in Perugia," and that was a mistake on my part. He definitely shares blame for the smear campaign put forth against Amanda Knox early on and like Vogt and Nadeau he continues to push many of the same lies.

Follain reports for the Rupert Murdoch owned *Times of London,* and has also written a book on the case. Follain's publisher Hodder & Stoughton delayed the release of his book about the Amanda Knox case three times since it had first graced Amazon's UK website before finally releasing it October 25, 2011. Funny that a book titled "Death in Perugia: The Definitive Account of the Killing of Meredith Kercher" was delayed so many times all while claiming to be "definitive."

Follain is known for his chummy relationship with prosecutors and the police involved in the Amanda Knox case, seen by several court observers frequently whispering in their ears during court sessions. Follain's close ties with police got him into Capanne prison, where he tried to speak with Amanda, who refused (he interviewed her cell mate instead).

Follain, who as late as March 2011 told readers that, "Contamination is in theory always possible but I see nothing to indicate that happened here," and concluded that Amanda Knox's appeal would go the same way as her original trial. Had Follain listened to anyone other than police and prosecutors, perhaps he would not have been so blindsided by the details emerging on appeal that likely caused his book to be delayed.

The *Times of London*, at one time one of the United Kingdom's most prestigious papers, has allowed Follain to nurture his ridiculous tabloid sensibilities. For instance, in September 2008, Follain wrote an article headlined "Amanda Knox, 'Foxy Knoxy', reveals her lesbian trauma." The story here was that Amanda had mentioned to Raffaele that some of her high school classmates thought she might be a lesbian, because she had helped a gay male friend set up an organization for gay students.

Since Follain began covering the case, his obsession with Amanda and her sex life has exposed a Madonna/whore complex unmatched even by London's sleaziest tabloids the *Mirror* and the *Sun*. Thanks to

Follain, trashy headlines never failed to accompany an article about Amanda Knox in the Times:

"Amanda Knox snared by her lust and her lies"

"Foxy Knoxy the 'she-devil' waits serene"

"Diary reveals Foxy Knoxy's sex secrets"

In December, 2009, on the day of the verdict, Follain put forth the absurd assertion that the relationship between Amanda and Meredith had soured because "it appears that it was Amanda's sex life that really drove a wedge between the women" even though both were sexually active at the time and no evidence was presented that Meredith ever said anything negative about Amanda's sex life. Additionally, Follain asserted the oft repeated lie that Amanda brought home "strange men" to the cottage where her and Meredith lived, even though at trial it was shown that Amanda had very few visitors, and all the visitors were known to Meredith.

Incidentally, in the same article on the day of the verdict, Follain quoted blogger Peggy Ganong, stating that she was an "Italian-speaking" Seattle blogger and quoting her where she said: "The implication was that all Italian forensics are inferior to American forensics, and I think that's just not true. The forensic evidence was a lot stronger than her supporters said". Of course, Follain failed to mention that Ganong could not speak Italian, had no experience in forensics, had never been to Perugia, and was administrator of an Amanda Knox hate site. Peggy Ganong is discussed further in the next chapter.

Perhaps what Follain is most well known for is writing the June 15, 2008 article with an interview of Amanda's parents Curt Knox and Edda Mellas, which prompted the police to charge both with criminal slander simply for repeating what Amanda had told them about being hit during her interrogation. Curt Knox stated: "Amanda was abused physically and verbally. She told us she was hit in the back of the head by a police officer with an open hand, at least twice. The police told her, 'If you ask for a lawyer, things will get worse for you' and 'If you don't give us some explanation for what happened, you're going to go to jail for a very long time."

Incidentally, in this same article, Follain made egregious errors in describing a story about rape that Amanda Knox had posted on her Myspace page. Follain summarized it as a story in "which a young woman drugs and rapes another woman" and quoted from it as follows: "She fell on the floor; she felt the blood on her mouth and swallowed it. She couldn't move her jaw and felt as if someone was moving a razor on the left side of her face."

Follain completely misrepresented the story, suggesting that it glorifies rape. In fact, the story is about the relationship between two brothers, one of whom accuses the other of drugging and raping a girl. This leads to a physical altercation between the brothers, described as follows: "Edgar dropped to the floor and tasted the blood in his mouth and swallowed it. He couldn't move his jaw and it felt like someone was jabbing a razor into the left side of his face." This story has been available online ever since Amanda and Raffaele were arrested. Why did Follain alter the text? Perhaps he did so because an accurate description of the story would not have the lurid and incriminating spin he wanted to convey to his readers.

If Follain's journalistic efforts have shown us anything, accuracy is not his strong suit. Keep that in mind if you plan on reading his newly released book.

There are many in the media that owe Amanda and Raffaele an apology but I doubt that we will hear from them anytime soon. The journalists that reported false information will continue to repeat Pisa's excuse saying they were not at fault early on due to the fact that much of the information they reported came directly from the prosecution's office. The media will forever own part of the blame in this tragedy, and that blame must not casually be deferred; but there is no doubt that Prosecutor Mignini worked hard to manipulate the media during the first trial by leaking false information to the press to benefit his case. The journalists mentioned in this chapter essentially became mouthpieces for his agenda. Even though Mignini was not the prosecutor leading the appeal, he was retained as assistant counsel, as often happens in high profile cases such as this in Italy, so he was still very much a part of this case throughout the appeal.

Thankfully, the media that Mignini worked hard to manipulate would not be as kind to him the second time around. During the appeal, Mignini stumbled when giving information to the press revealing his true feelings about the case and casting doubt on his theories. Mignini's blunders occurred during two separate interviews; one with CNN and the other with Bob Graham, a British journalist for the *Sun* tabloid. When

Mignini agreed to be interviewed he was opening a door into his thoughts that he may now wish remained closed.

CNN interviewed Mignini for a Documentary airing in May, 2011, titled *"Murder Abroad: The Amanda Knox Story – CNN's Drew Griffin Reports."* This interview turned out to be an embarrassing one for Mignini as he seemed to stumble through the questions in a state of confusion. According to Griffin, Mignini was focused more on Amanda than the case itself, often bringing information about Amanda into the conversation that had nothing to do with the trial. Griffin told Candace Dempsey that Mignini's rambling was "the kind of things that, if a prosecutor came to court in the U.S. and put before a judge, would get his whole case thrown out." At the end of the interview Mignini apparently knew that he did not fare well because he later approached Griffin on the street asking him if he sounded truthful. Mignini's CNN interview may have left viewers to wonder about his wellbeing but his truly shocking statements would come shortly thereafter during an interview with Bob Graham.

Bob Graham interviewed Mignini on May 21, 2011. In that interview, Mignini would admit for the first time that no trace of Amanda Knox was found at the crime scene. It took nearly four years for Mignini to come clean with this fact. No problem for Mignini because, as we have seen time and time again, Mignini's theories change often. In his newest theory Amanda orchestrated the murder from another room! Really? Mignini describes as follows:

> *"Amanda might theoretically have instigated the murder while even staying in the other room"*

Mignini's statements in this interview were crucial because he contradicted the reasoning for Amanda's conviction. Amanda was convicted on the basis that she had a dual role in the murder. We were told that she not only masterminded but also participated in the attack.

To further discredit his leadership in the first trial, Mignini claimed that the crime scene was not thoroughly investigated because there was not enough time. He used this excuse to further justify why there were no traces of Amanda and Raffaele at the crime scene. Not enough time? Who is he kidding? Amanda and Raffaele sat in prison for a year before even being charged with a crime. Mignini had more than enough time to investigate the crime. No traces were found because Amanda and Raffaele were not there. Maybe if we wait long enough Mignini will come completely clean and admit that too.

It was nice to see Mignini being exposed by the same media that he once manipulated for his own benefit. Unfortunately, Mignini has managed to hold onto his position of power even though he has been convicted of abuse of power in another case. He continues to abuse that power (more to come) and will do so until the day he is relieved of his duties as prosecutor.

It was very encouraging to finally see a majority of the media more accurately reporting the truth about this case during the appeal, but it was even more encouraging to see good investigative reporting revealing unknown details as well.

There are a few journalists that have stood above all others when it comes to professional coverage of this case. Candace Dempsey, Nikki Battiste, Elizabeth Vargas, Steve Shay, Linda Byron, and Doug Longhini in the United States as well as Bob Graham and Peter

Popham in the United Kingdom, are on the top of my list. This small list of journalists has consistently avoided taking the easy route of latching onto the pack, and by doing so has shown that quality journalism is still alive and well. These journalists deserve high praise for their integrity and hard work. To this small group, reporting the truth outweighed thinking about their own personal gain.

It might not sound like much to ask for journalists to properly research topics and then present their findings to the public, but in today's fast paced world where headlines have a very short shelf life, there is a lot of pressure to get the most bang for your buck. Unfortunately most journalists took the easy route for a majority of this case and have only shifted position because they are continuing to follow the pack as they have always done. Even though it has been refreshing to see the case being reported on truthfully in a more widespread fashion, the pack journalists deserve no praise for their proper coverage in the late stages of the trial.

The media coverage in Italy was showing slight promise but not nearly as promising as seen in the United States and the United Kingdom. As we know, Frank Sfarzo has been a courageous voice in Italy, refusing to be silenced even under extreme pressure. Giangavalo Sulas and Elio Bertoldi of *Oggi* magazine deserve praise for their coverage throughout this case as they have both been outspoken since the beginning. Several other news outlets in Italy were actively reporting on the ongoing appeal as well, but news about the case was not a hot topic like it had been during the first trial. Why were Italian journalists ignoring this case? Were Italians simply tired of hearing about it or were there other reasons for the notable lack of news coverage?

6

abuse of power

In April, 2011, the Committee to Protect Journalists (CPJ), an independent, nonpartisan organization dedicated to defending the rights of journalists worldwide, provided a very good reason for the glaring lack of coverage of the Meredith Kercher murder case by Italian journalists in Perugia, Italy.

In an open letter to Italian President Giorgio Napolitano, CPJ expressed great concern for journalists who have been harassed by authorities and even jailed for speaking out about the case against Amanda Knox and Raffaele Sollecito in Perugia, Italy.

CPJ was especially concerned with the conduct of Prosecutor Giuliano Mignini. CPJ reports that the anti-press actions of Mignini and those under his supervision caused the press to shy away from reporting on the Meredith Kercher case including the appeal trial for Amanda Knox and Raffaele Sollecito. They reported that pressure was put on local reporters and individual bloggers who did not have the backing of large news organizations. They noted that these individuals were most vulnerable to retaliation, including prosecution and physical attack.

The open letter highlighted the abuse of freelance reporter Frank Sfarzo, who was and continues to be very critical of the case on his blog Perugia Shock. The details that came to light about the abuse suffered by Frank were startling. According to Frank, police regularly tried to prevent him from entering the courthouse, often harassing him on the street. Once inside the courtroom, insults were mouthed at him and officers stared over his shoulder as he took notes.

Frank said the harassment escalated when police forcibly entered his apartment without producing a warrant or showing their badges. Four of the five shoved him to the ground, struck him, handcuffed him, and climbed on top of him, crushing his air supply. Police then took him to the Perugia city hospital, where they claimed he had attacked them. Police attempted to persuade a doctor to issue a medical report for the injuries he was alleged to have caused the police. Frank was then brought before a psychiatrist, where the police demanded that he be diagnosed insane. Police told the doctor that Frank was pathologically obsessed with the case, being so fixated on it that he must be insane. Thankfully for Frank, the psychiatrist refused to comply with the officer's request.

Frank's ordeal did not end at the hospital. Officers took him to the police station and in Frank's words: "they displayed me as a trophy," referring to him as "the bastard who defends Amanda Knox." Frank's requests to call his lawyer or relatives were denied and he spent the night in a jail cell. Frank was released pending a trial where he could face up to six years in prison. At the time of this writing, Frank's case was still pending.

The open letter from the CPJ may very well answer the question as to why the media coverage of this case has been minimal in Italy compared to coverage seen throughout the world.

It is well documented that Giuliano Mignini, the man in charge of the campaign to manipulate the media, not only relied on threats of physical violence but also abused the power of his office to threaten legal action against his detractors. As discussed in *Injustice in Perugia*, Mignini filed defamation charges on no less than a dozen people, including Amanda's parents and even her attorneys. What is most disturbing is that Mignini abused his power while he was under investigation for abuse in a previous trial. Shortly after the Amanda Knox case reached a verdict, Mignini found himself convicted.

To give a brief recap, Mignini was convicted in Florence of abusing his official powers while investigating the death of Dr. Francesco Narducci in relation to the Monster of Florence case. Mignini was sentenced to 16 months in prison. Normal procedure in Italian criminal justice allows him to live his life and carry on—business as usual—until his appeal is heard. This freedom also allows him to continue to prosecute cases. Mignini described the charges against him as technical and difficult to understand. But the charges are not confusing at all: Mignini abused the power of his office.

Mignini was convicted of illegally investigating journalists who had criticized him. The court found that Mignini had targeted Italian journalists because they had criticized his investigation of Narducci's death. Mignini was also convicted on two separate charges of ordering illegal investigations. These illegal investigations targeted the Florentine ex-police chief Giuseppe De Donno as well as two officials of the Viminale (the Ministry of the Interior in Rome), including Roberto Sgalla, former director of the office of external affairs.

These investigations were unlawful because they involved illegal wiretaps. Mignini also created investigative files for his targets without proper approval. The court determined that his investigations were designed to "harass and intimidate" people who had criticized him or Chief Inspector Michele Giuttari for their conduct during the Narducci investigation.

The charges against Mignini are serious. Some members of the media have reported that these charges are simply administrative. This is not the case. Mignini was given a sixteen-month prison sentence, six months more than the prosecutor asked for. However, he is unlikely to see jail time and his sentence is suspended while his case is on appeal.

Unfortunately, Mignini will most likely never spend any time in jail. However, his career is in serious jeopardy. If his conviction is upheld, he will be removed from public office and will no longer be allowed to serve as a prosecutor or judge. His career will be over. Mignini's appeal is scheduled for November 2011.

Until Mignini's conviction is confirmed, there is little chance that he will stop abusing his power. Mignini made it clear that he was not swayed by CPJ's concerns regarding his past and present behavior, when he pressed forward with a defamation lawsuit against Perugia Shock, a blog created and maintained by Frank Sfarzo. Mignini repeatedly threatened legal action throughout the course of the first trial in an attempt to silence those who disagreed with him so his abusive conduct shown toward Frank was not a shock.

Unfortunately, Google bowed to Mignini's pressure and took Frank's blog offline. Frank told CPJ that he received an email from Google, which hosted the Perugia Shock blog, informing him that a court order has been issued for the "preventive closure" of his blog. It was from that court order that Frank learned that Mignini had filed a lawsuit against Perugia Shock for "defamation, carried out by means of a website." The court order was issued on February 23, by Florentine Judge Paola Belsino.

Injustice in Perugia felt that it was crucial that Frank Sfarzo's reporting was not silenced. We had frequently backed up the Perugia Shock blog because we long feared that it would become a target of Mignini. The day Frank's blog went offline, Jason Leznek, one of IIP's core members, began recreating a new Perugia Shock blog on WordPress.

Frank Sfarzo is the only reporter to attend every single court hearing for Amanda Knox and Raffaele

Sollecito, and the only Italian reporter that provided information to an English speaking audience. Perugia Shock has provided invaluable first hand information about this case for nearly four years. Frank Sfarzo's voice would not be silenced by a corrupt prosecutor hell-bent on destroying anyone who dared to disagree with him. Enough was enough!

The Committee to Protect Journalists was appalled to see Mignini blatantly abuse the powers of his office and was quick to respond:

"The Committee to Protect Journalists authorities calls on Florence and Perugia to drop the trumped-up defamation lawsuit against Perugia Shock, an English-language blog created and maintained by Frank Sfarzo, an Italian freelance journalist and blogger. Sfarzo has endured sustained harassment in retaliation for his reporting and commentary on the official investigation into the November 2007 murder of British exchange student Meredith Kercher."

"We call on Perugia Prosecutor Giuliano Mignini to drop his defamation lawsuit against Perugia Shock and allow it to remain online," CPJ Europe and Central Asia Program Coordinator Nina Ognianova said. "This is hardly the first time Mignini has resorted to the law to silence his critics. It's a heavy-handed tactic that is bound to have a chilling effect on journalists in Italy."

Frank Sfarzo's abuse was a hot topic on blogs that follow the Amanda Knox case. You would think that other bloggers would have come to Frank Sfarzo's defense, in light of the fact that his blog was taken offline, as this was clearly a matter of free speech. Instead the Anti-Knox groups took the opportunity to attack Frank Sfarzo and CPJ. The true intention of these groups was crystal clear in their reaction to this story. I would ask anyone who ever looked to the Anti-Knox sites for information, to ask themselves, what kind of person would condone the harassment of a journalist or a blogger, no matter what side of this debate he or she stands on?

Frank Sfarzo deserves the support of anyone who believes in the right to free speech. Those who fought so hard against him need to stop and think about what they were actually fighting for

Giuliano Mignini may have thought he was successful in silencing Frank Sfarzo when Google took Perugia Shock offline, but Mignini was sadly mistaken if he thought Perugia Shock would remain silenced for long. Frank was back online within a few days and continues blogging to this day.

Italy needs to deal with Giuliano Mignini. It is an embarrassment to Italy that he still holds onto his power and it is only a matter of time before he abuses the power of his office again. It is the only way he knows how to conduct his business.

7

Meredith Kercher's killer takes the stand

After another long delay, the eighth appeal hearing was held on June 18 2011 (day 1321). This hearing was not short on drama as five prison inmates would take the stand in defense of Amanda and Raffaele. These inmates were called to testify about prison yard conversations they had with Meredith Kercher's killer, Rudy Guede.

Guede's conversations were significant because he repeatedly stated that Amanda and Raffaele were not present at the crime scene when Meredith Kercher was murdered. It was shocking to see the defense calling on a convicted child killer to testify but that is exactly what they did when they put Mario Alessi on the stand. Alessi told the court that he was friends with Guede in prison and he spoke of conversations that he and Guede shared in the prison yard where Guede told him that Amanda and Raffaele were innocent. According to Alessi, Guede told him that he and another man murdered Meredith Kercher.

It is understandable to ask why a jury would believe the testimony of a convicted child killer. The man is a repulsive human being. However, the defense also brought in three additional inmates to corroborate that Guede told them the same story. It would be very difficult for the three to keep details straight during questioning if there was no truth to the story. Importantly, the testimony showed that Guede stated repeatedly that Amanda and Raffaele were innocent.

Another inmate, well known mobster, Luciano Aviello, also testified but his story was far from that of the others. He told the court that his brother Antonio murdered Meredith Kercher. According to Aviello, his brother came home to the residence they shared to inform him that he stabbed Meredith after entering her apartment to steal a painting he thought was there. Aviello told the court that his brother's jacket was torn and he was covered in blood. He claimed that is brother asked him to help hide a set of keys and a knife used in the murder.

Aviello wrote to the court several times about his brother's alleged involvement but was never questioned. In the case of Aviello, the fact that he was never questioned by authorities was more important than his actual testimony because the court had an obligation to exhaust all possibilities and in this case they failed to do so. It showed that the prosecution cherry picked witnesses that fit their theory and ignored those who contradicted it. Antonio Curatolo was a good example of this. Why did they extensively interview a homeless drug addict and completely ignore Aviello?

As expected, both witnesses were completely unreliable. As we know Curatolo was embarrassed on appeal, and as it turned out, Aviello later admitted that his claims were fabricated. The defense did not buy Aviello's story but by calling him to testify, the court saw firsthand how the prosecution selectively sorted through the witness list, a clear violation of Italian law.

The defense move to put the inmates on the stand prompted the prosecution to request that Rudy Guede be called to testify to refute the allegations made by the inmates. This request was granted by the court and Guede took the stand during the 9th hearing held on June 27, 2011. It was understandable that the prosecution wanted to generate some kind of response to the inmate testimony but calling Guede was a long shot. Guede lied repeatedly throughout this case, modifying his stories, based on news reports as it best suited his defense, meaning anything he said on the stand would lack credibility.

Guede was recorded during a Skype conversation before his arrest telling a friend that the reports on the news were incorrect. He said Amanda Knox was not present the night the crime took place. After his arrest Guede realized he had no way out and repeatedly modified his story to help his own defense. His latest story suggests he was being intimate with Meredith in her room when he suddenly needed to use the bathroom. While he was in the bathroom Amanda and Raffaele came in and murdered Meredith. Of course, none of his stories were accepted as his conviction has been finalized by the Italian Supreme Court.

Guede's attorneys did an excellent job of securing the most lenient punishment possible for his crime by convincing the court that Guede was merely an accomplice. Guede received a reduced sentence of 16 years on appeal, of which he will only serve a fraction, leaving many years of freedom in his future. The sad truth is that Guede will be eligible for work release in 2015.

How can I say with complete certainty that Rudy Guede murdered Meredith Kercher? Unlike Amanda and Raffaele, Guede was arrested after the evidence collected at the crime scene was analyzed and that evidence points right to him—no one else, just him. There was no rush to judgment when it came to arresting Rudy Guede. Investigators found Guede's hand print on a pillow case found under the victim's body. The fingerprints led police to their suspect. When the police came looking for Guede, he had already fled to Germany. Thankfully, old fashioned police work nabbed Guede; he was stopped in Germany trying to board a train without a ticket and was immediately extradited back to Italy.

The evidence of Guede's guilt is irrefutable and should have been more than sufficient to secure a life sentence. Guede admitted he was in Meredith's room at the time of the attack. His DNA, along with Meredith's blood, was found on Meredith's purse. His shoeprints, set in Meredith's blood, were found in the bedroom and in the hallway leading out the front door. As mentioned above, his handprint, in Meredith's blood, was found on a pillowcase underneath her body. Most importantly, Guede's DNA was found inside Meredith's body.

Guede also had a history of break-ins similar to that seen at the cottage. One week prior to the murder, Guede was caught breaking into a nursery school by the school's owner, Maria Del Prato, when she arrived unexpectedly during off hours with two repairmen. Del Prato along with the repairmen kept Guede at the nursery and called the police.

When police searched Guede's backpack they found a laptop and cell phone that had recently been stolen from a Perugian law office. The break-in at the law office was very similar to the break-in at the cottage as Guede entered through an elevated window broken with a rock in both occasions. In the nursery school break-in, Guede was found in the possession of a large knife said to be stolen from the school's kitchen. He was also in possession of a woman's gold watch which tied him to another break-in occurring four days earlier. Guede's break-in at the nursery no doubt made him a suspect in a previous burglary of the nursery in which cash had been stolen.

In the month prior to Meredith Kercher's murder, Guede had gone on a crime spree. His activities were no secret to the police yet they never managed to properly investigate Guede and never took him into custody. Why? The sad reality is, if the police had done their job properly Meredith Kercher would still be alive today and Amanda Knox and Raffaele Sollecito would have never been wrongfully convicted.

Despite police negligence, why did the court ignore Guede's behavior during the first trial? All evidence at the crime scene pointed to him and he had a history of similar break-ins yet the prosecution was hell-bent on fitting Amanda and Raffaele into the scenario. Why was it so difficult for the police to admit they made a mistake? So many questions that needed answers but unfortunately those answers would never come. With all that is known about Guede, there was little surprise that tension was high when he entered the court room on June 27 2011, in the presence of Amanda and Raffaele.

Guede had nothing to gain or lose (with regard to his prison sentence) by testifying at Amanda and Raffaele's appeal, but he did have an opportunity to do what's right; he had the opportunity to actually tell the truth. Guede will never be able to correct the damage he has caused but he could have shown that he had an ounce of humanity left in his soul by stopping the destruction of two additional lives by informing the court that his accusations against Amanda and Raffaele were nothing more than lies. Even though Guede risked no additional prison time by telling the truth, given his character, it was highly unlikely that we would ever confess to the truth.

When Guede entered the courtroom he seemed to make an effort to avoid any eye contact with Amanda and Raffaele. As soon as Guede had stated his name and sat down, Amanda immediately stood up while her attorney announced to the court that Amanda wanted to make a statement. Amanda had the right to face her accuser and question them according to Italian law. Judge Hellmann, for reasons not explained, denied her that right, and said she could speak after Guede had finished with his testimony and was no longer in the courtroom.

As expected, Guede's testimony reiterated his latest story about Amanda and Raffaele that he had written in a letter in 2010. The letter was produced to the court by Prosecutor Giuliano Mignini. After the judge had reviewed the letter and handed it to Guede, Mignini asked Guede to read it out loud to the court. After a short pause, Guede said no. When Mignini asked him why, Guede claimed to be unable to read his own handwriting.

In a strange courtroom display, his letter was then read aloud by Mignini. Judge Zanetti found this odd prompting him to ask Guede if he understood the words written in the letter, as it contained many words that only a lawyer would think to use. Zanetti asked Guede about his education level, and if he knew the definition of the words in question. Guede said he knew them all, and that he had completed middle school, and would not go any farther into the debate. This odd moment left many feeling that Guede was being guided on what to say regarding Amanda and Raffaele. Did this guidance have anything to do with Guede's lenient prison term? As we have come to realize, many questions in Perugia never receive answers.

As Mignini read the words allegedly penned by Guede, the court heard Guede's accusation that Amanda and Raffaele murdered Meredith Kercher. Old news or not, hearing these words while Guede was in the same courtroom was shocking to Amanda and Raffaele none the less. Amanda gave an emotional declaration to the court once Guede had been shuffled out:

> *"Please the Court, I simply want to declare that the only time that Rudy Guede, Raffaele and I were together in the same space is in a courtroom. We never had any kind of contact. I am shocked and anguished by his declarations, truly, because he*

*knows it, that we weren't there. He knows that we
weren't involved and I don't know what happened that
night. I just wish I could tell him 'Look, mistakes can
be fixed by first telling the truth.' That's all. Thank
you."*

Raffaele also passionately addressed the court showing
disgust that he was unable to face his accuser.

> *"Rudy said in his chat to Giacomo Benedetti that
> Amanda wasn't there, and as a male he saw just a
> shadow. Then he accused us just because we were
> already blamed!"*

> *"For almost four years I'm fighting against the
> shadows, and he comes here, and doesn't even
> speak. What should I defend myself from, if he
> doesn't speak?"*

Although Guede's testimony was dramatized by the
media it actually went exactly as expected. No one
imagined that Guede would come clean and tell the truth.
He did answer my question as to whether or not he had a
conscience; the answer is clearly no.

Even though the media improved drastically as the
appeal progressed, it had to be expected that details of
Guede's testimony would be simply too irresistible for
even the most disciplined reporters to not exaggerate.
Unfortunately this led to another round of sensationalized
headlines and misrepresentation of the facts, suggesting
to the public that Guede provided shocking new
information. It's okay; the headlines carried no weight

and quickly faded away leaving Guede's testimony to have no lasting effect on the trial.

When it was all said and done, there was no real way to gauge whether or not the defense needed to call the inmates in to testify. They did achieve their goal of highlighting how the witnesses were wrongly handled by the prosecution during the first trial but it took two full court hearings in a circus like environment to achieve that goal. Either way, there was certainly nothing negative to come from it other than possibly causing unneeded distraction for the jurors. Coming events would prevent any distraction from being a problem for the defense. The court had everyone's full attention during the next hearing when the forensic experts appointed by Judge Hellmann came to testify.

8

independent experts set the record straight

July 25, 2011 (day 1358), was a very important day for Amanda and Raffaele as forensic experts Stefano Conti and Carla Vecchiotti, from Rome's Sapienza University arrived in court armed with laptops, a projector, and piles of paperwork, detailing their analysis of the DNA evidence that would ultimately decide the fate of Amanda and Raffaele. It is important to keep in mind that Conti and Vecchiotti were appointed by the court. Many news outlets reported that they were defense experts, which was not the case.

Conti and Vecchiotti were given the job of providing an unbiased analysis of the DNA evidence presented at the first trial. When Judge Hellmann appointed Conti and Vecchiotti, he was essentially giving them the power to decide the future of Amanda and Raffaele. Injustice in Perugia has repeatedly stated throughout the course of the trial that the truth would eventually prevail. This philosophy has had its critics due to the events that have been witnessed throughout this case but Conti and Vecchiotti's testimony would go a long way to show that the power of truth was still alive and well.

In a major victory for the defense, Conti and Vecchiotti concluded that the alleged murder weapon and the DNA laden bra clasp used to convict Amanda and Raffaele were unreliable and cited multiple errors made by investigators. Conti and Vecchiotti's testimony was especially critical of the prosecution's forensic expert Patrizia Stefanoni who not only supervised the evidence collection at the cottage but also conducted the analysis at the lab.

Conti and Vecchiotti's testimony was described as "shocking" as sound bites of their scathing criticism blazed through news outlets worldwide, and though it may have been shocking to casual followers, for many it came nearly four years too late.

A recap of the knife: The knife was the prosecution's "smoking gun" said to have Amanda's DNA on the handle and Meredith's DNA on the blade. An investigator claimed he retrieved the knife from

Raffaele's kitchen drawer because it looked clean. Investigators neglected to test any other knives from either Raffaele's kitchen or the kitchen at the location of the murder, quickly concluding they had found the murder weapon. The knife was suspect from the start not only because of how it was found but also because it was too large to cause Meredith's fatal wounds and did not match a bloody imprint of a knife found on Meredith's bed sheet.

Conti and Vecchiotti's conclusion: There was no blood on the knife, no DNA from the victim, no evidence whatsoever to show that the knife was involved in any way. They did confirm Amanda's DNA on the handle which was expected because she used the knife for cooking at Raffaele's apartment. Conti and Vecchiotti also discovered starch from rye bread on the knife blade which was consistent with the fact that it was used for cooking. Conti and Vecchiotti's analysis was far more powerful than any defense expert could present because it came from an independent voice, appointed by the court. The truth was finally crystal clear; the knife in question was not the murder weapon.

A recap of the bra clasp: The clasp was horribly mishandled by investigators and should have never been admissible as evidence in the first place. The defense experts did an excellent job of discrediting the clasp during the first trial but their analysis was ignored. Just like the knife evidence, the damming analysis would be heard from independent voices on appeal, and these voices would not be ignored.

The prosecution claimed the clasp, which was torn from Kercher's bra during the attack, contained

Raffaele's DNA. No other evidence linked either Raffaele or Amanda to the murder room making the clasp vital to the prosecution's case. Several factors discredit this piece of evidence. Investigators neglected to collect the clasp for 47 days leaving it to be shuffled around on the floor as seen in crime scene video throughout that time frame. When the clasp was finally collected, multiple investigators handled it with contaminated gloves. Conti and Vecchiotti detailed the clear negligence witnessed during the evidence collection but more importantly, they reported that Patrizia Stefanoni erroneously interpreted the electrophoretic profile when she concluded that Raffaele's DNA was present on the clasp.

The method Stefanoni used centers in on a specific suspect, a practice that is forbidden by all international standards due to the fact that it leads to biased analysis. Samples are to be analyzed individually and then the final results are compared to see if any produce a positive match. If one begins knowing what they are looking for already, they are likely to interpret the electorpherogram to match the result they are trying to achieve. Conti and Vecchiotti explain as follows:

> *"Statements about a profile obtained from a sample under examination, regarding the decision as to which is a true allele and which a 'drop-in', must necessarily be pronounced without knowledge of the suspect's profile; only in such a way, in fact, can a qualitatively unimpeachable and balanced approach to the interpretation of the profile emerging from the sample in question be guaranteed. An interpretation of the profile obtained from a sample, carried out*

*with the suspect's reference profile available,
indicates an imbalanced [approach], and is in total
contrast with the absolutely objective nature of
forensic science"*

Stefanoni not only violated protocol, but also lied about it in court when she stated that she had adhered to proper procedure and analyzed all traces in an absolutely objective manner. Her boss, Dr. Renato Biondo, head of the DNA Unit at Polizia Scientifica, Rome, and consultant for the prosecution, needed positive results from Stefanoni and she was more than willing to fulfill the request.

Stefanoni lied in court again, claiming that stains detected at the crime scene using luminol (an investigative tool used to detect blood not visible to the human eye) were never tested for blood; however, in July 2009, when pressured by the defense, Stefanoni released information originally withheld confirming the stains were tested with tetramethylbenzidine, which is extremely sensitive for blood. All of the stains detected with luminol tested negative for blood. Stefanoni held this information from the court testifying instead that the stains were indeed blood. This is yet another example where Stefanoni created evidence to benefit the prosecution.

But Stefanoni's lies do not end there. She also lied when she testified that she changed gloves every time she handled a new sample. However, Raffaele Sollecito's defense used clear video and photographic evidence to show that Stefanoni used the same gloves multiple times while collecting samples. This lie was highlighted once again by Conti and Vecchiotti during the appeal.

It is clear that much of the blame belongs to Patrizia Stefanoni, who lied repeatedly in court to benefit the prosecution. The independent experts cited egregious violations committed by Stefanoni that clearly shows she had an agenda.

It is shocking that police negligence did not play a much larger role in the first trial. Much of the evidence collection was captured on video and many cases of faulty procedure and quite frankly odd behavior can be viewed throughout the entire collection process.

Conti and Vecchiotti used video taken during evidence collection in court to show negligence. Testimony from Stefanoni defending her work was read to the court followed by video clips showing that she was being less than honest in her own defense. The examples of negligence were so ridiculous that the court burst out in laughter on several occasions during the presentation. It is hard to imagine that anyone could actually laugh out loud during a serious trial such as this, but sometimes things are so absurd that laughter is the only possible emotion.

When I viewed the evidence collection videos I noted several procedures that seemed strange to me, but there was one that stood high above the rest. In an odd sight to see, Stefanoni is seen wrapping a mop handle in gift wrap (that she retrieved from the closet containing the mop) only to hand it off to another investigator so she can parade it around the cottage. Why did they gift wrap a mop and walk it around the cottage?

So what's the big deal about the mop? First, gift wrap is not a proper collection tool, second, the mop head was left exposed as the investigator (for reasons I cannot imagine) walked the mop into the murder room where the

most crucial evidence was collected. For me the gift wrap is more symbolic of how this case played out.
Investigators had the job of collecting gifts for Prosecutor Giuliano Mignini who in turn used those gifts to create a well packaged series of lies to be offered to the court. Sadly the plan worked causing irreparable damage to two innocent people.

The truth is investigators completely mishandled the crime scene causing much of the evidence to be susceptible to contamination. More importantly, the court accepted the evidence, leading to the wrongful conviction of Amanda Knox and Raffaele Sollecito.

Here is an English translation of the conclusions reached by the independent court appointed experts Stefano Conti and Carla Vecchiotti.

CONCLUSIONS
Based on the considerations explained above, we are able to respond as follows to the inquiries posed at the assignment hearing:

Having examined the record and conducted such technical investigations as shall be necessary, the Expert Panel shall ascertain:

1. Whether it is possible, by means of a new technical analysis, to identify the DNA present on items 165b (bra clasp) and 36 (knife), and to determine the reliability of any such identification"

-The tests that we conducted to determine the presence of blood on item 36 (knife) and item 165B (bra clasps) yielded a negative result.

The cytomorphological tests on the items did not reveal the presence of cellular material. Some samples of item 36 (knife), in particular sample "H", present granules with a circular/hexagonal characteristic morphology with a cental radial structure. A more detailed microscopic study, together with the consultation of data in the literature, allowed us to ascertain that the structures in question are attributable to granules of starch, thus matter of a vegetable nature.

- The quantification of the extracts obtained from the samples obtained from item 36 (knife) and item 165B (bra clasps), conducted via Real Time PCR, did not reveal the presence of DNA.

- In view of the absence of DNA in the extracts that we obtained, with the agreement of the consultants for the parties, we did not proceed to the subsequent amplification step.

2. if it is not possible to carry out a new technical analysis, shall evaluate, on the basis of the record, the degree of reliability of the genetic analysis performed by the Scientific Police on the aforementioned items, including with respect to possible contamination.

Having examined the record and the relevant documents, we are able to report the following conclusions regarding the laboratory analyses performed on Item 36 (knife) and Item 165B (bra clasps):

ITEM 36 (KNIFE)

Relative to the genetic analysis performed on trace A (handle of the knife), we agree with the conclusion reached by the Technical Consultant regarding the attribution of the genetic profile obtained from these samples to Amanda Marie Knox.

Relative to trace B (blade of the knife) we find that the technical analyses performed are not reliable for the following reasons:

1. There does not exist evidence which scientifically confirms that trace B (blade of knife) is the product of blood.

2. The electrophoretic profiles exhibited reveal that the sample indicated by the letter B (blade of knife) was a Low Copy Number (LCN) sample, and, as such, all of the precautions indicated by the international scientific community should have been applied.

3. Taking into account that none of the recommendations of the international scientific community relative to the treatment of Low Copy Number (LCN) samples were followed, we do not accept the conclusions regarding the certain attribution of the profile found on trace B (blade of knife) to the victim Meredith Susanna Cara Kercher, since the genetic profile, as obtained, appears unreliable insofar as it is not supported by scientifically validated analysis;

4. International protocols of inspection, collection,

and sampling were not followed;

5. It cannot be ruled out that the result obtained from sample B (blade of knife) derives from contamination in some phase of the collection and/or handling and/or analyses performed.

ITEM 165B (BRA CLASPS)
Relative to Item 165B (bra clasps), we find that the technical analysis is not reliable for the following reasons:

1. There does not exist evidence which scientifically confirms the presence of supposed flaking cells on the item;

2. There was an erroneous interpretation of the electrophoretic profile of the autosomic STRs;

3. There was an erroneous interpretation of the electrophoretic profile relative to the Y chromosome;

4. The international protocols for inspection, collection, and sampling of the item were not followed;

5. It cannot be ruled out that the results obtained derive from environmental contamination and/or contamination in some phase of the collection and/or handling of the item.

These conclusions have been reached by Professor

Carla Vecchiotti and Professor Stefano Conti.

For many onlookers, the testimony of Conti and Vecchiotti was all that was needed to see that Amanda and Raffaele were innocent, but unfortunately more delays would be endured by the two before closing arguments would begin. Italian courts shut down during the summer allowing for a summer recess, with court resuming in the middle of September. Judge Hellmann would end up cutting the recess short by calling everyone back to court on September 5, only slightly helping the long delay.

In the meantime, the summer break gave me an opportunity to take a closer look at several other aspects revolving around the case.

Amanda Knox in 2007 before leaving for Italy.
Photograph courtesy of Friends of Amanda.

Raffaele Sollecito pictured in court during an appeal hearing. Photograph by Joseph Bishop.

The cottage where Meredith Kercher was murdered.
Photograph by Joseph Bishop.

Giuliano Mignini's reaction at the exact moment that
Judge Hellmann declared Amanda and Raffaele innocent.
Photograph by Mario Spezi.

Amanda Knox's attorney Luciano Ghirga taking questions outside the courthouse. Photograph by Joseph Bishop.

Steve Moore in Florence, Italy, two days before the verdict. Photograph courtesy of Steve Moore.

John Follain (seen in light colored jacket) listening to
Luciano Ghirga answer questions. Photograph by Joseph
Bishop.

Supporters for Amanda and Raffaele gathered for an all night vigil in Seattle, WA, waiting anxiously for the verdicts to be read. Photograph by Jim Lovering.

Supporters awaiting the verdict at the all night vigil in Seattle, WA. Photograph by Jim Lovering.

Rocco Girlanda hugs Amanda Knox as she leaves the Capanne prison for the last time. Photograph courtesy of the Italy–USA Foundation.

Amanda is seen holding Italy-USA foundation secretary general Corrado Daclon's hand as the vehicle she is being escorted in passes the gates of Capanne prison. Photograph courtesy of the Italy–USA Foundation.

9

the truth behind the hate campaign against Amanda Knox

The internet has certainly played a major role in the coverage of this case, leading me to write an entire chapter on the internet's influence in "Injustice in Perugia." During that discussion, I detailed a group of people that have actively campaigned against Amanda Knox online. Of course their anger has also been pointed at Raffaele but Amanda has always been the main target.

My initial approach was to limit the discussion to the general activities of the group, as I was reluctant to give those who were so adamantly against Amanda and Raffaele any more attention than necessary. As time went on it became crystal clear that these people were not simply campaigning to keep Amanda and Raffaele in prison, they were also actively trying to harm those who showed support for the two.

After seeing these hateful actions firsthand, my position changed drastically on how the pro-guilt group needed to be dealt with. I came to realize that it was very important for people to know what fueled the hate campaign against Amanda Knox.

The group I am referring to assembles on a website called Perugia Murder File (PMF). They also run a so called informational website called True Justice for Meredith Kercher.(TJMK). Seattle resident Peggy Ganong operates PMF. TJMK is run by New Jersey resident Peter Quennell.

Those who support TJMK/PMF are often referred to as pro-guilt, Anti-Knox, or guilters. Many names have been given to those who support Amanda and Raffaele as well. The most recent one would be FOAker, using the Friends of Amanda acronym.

The guilters have always claimed that their mission is to preserve the memory of Meredith Kercher but that is far from the truth. If I was going to set up a web site dedicated to a murder victim I would most likely look for ways to keep her memory alive such as setting up a college fund in her name or starting a charity to help victims of violence. To this day, the guilters have done absolutely nothing of the sort. There is a section on their website titled "Projects for Meredith" that is empty. Not one member in their group could think of anything they could do to honor the person they claimed to gather for Why? The answer to that question is simple; they do not really care about Meredith Kercher. Sure many casual readers that browse their site have deep sympathy for Meredith, (as any decent human being would have for anyone who had been so brutally murdered) but the core members of the group are far more interested in spewing hatred than doing anything in support of a murder victim.

Much of the hatred coming from the guilters has been spewed online. You will see this in comment sections of articles throughout the internet, in book reviews on Amazon.com, and in various blogs and commentaries. This online behavior is not unique to this case. People pop up on articles on all topics and post vile comments. That is the reality of anonymity online. Those comments are usually one and done, written simply for shock value. When you look closer at this case, you will see a far more organized effort. You will see that a group has actually come together with the sole purpose of destroying Amanda Knox.

The guilters mask their true intentions by pushing out so called experts to support their side of the argument. TJMK has run many featured articles promoting "exclusive expert analysis." It takes very little research to discover that these so called experts are complete frauds. One of these faux experts, Laura Wray, has already been discussed in the media chapter as an unreliable source used by Andrea Vogt. Wray posts on the pro-guilt sites proclaiming to be a forensic expert when in reality she works in the fashion industry. Here are a few more fraudulent characters that have been placed on pedestals by the guilters.

A guy named Peter Hyatt created a blog under the name Seamus O'Riley, in which he claims to be able to determine guilt or deception by reading the statements of others. He states on his blog that he determined that Amanda was guilty, just by reading her written statements. He also claims that he can determine that FBI Agent Steve Moore is deceptive in his support for Amanda's innocence. He is described in various places on the internet as an investigator for the State of Maine who works along with police departments in criminal investigations.

Of course Peter Quennell loves Hyatt and is more than happy to provide a platform for him on his website TJMK. The truth has never been important to Quennell and his followers. All you have to do to be accepted into Quennell's cult is to actively smear Amanda Knox, so it is no surprise that Hyatt is viewed as a hero on TJMK.

The truth is Hyatt is a complete fraud. He does not have a degree in statement analysis. Actually, his degree is in Bible Studies. He teaches guitar to children ages 5-12 and has a very respectable job of investigating complaints regarding the mistreatment of disabled people. He does not work at the "Laboratory for Statement Analysis for Scientific Interrogations" in Maine as he claimed. In fact, there is no such laboratory in the state of Maine.

Hyatt is not an expert and is not involved with any law enforcement agency. Hyatt is a guitar teacher. Do not get me wrong, I have absolutely nothing against guitar teachers; but I do have a problem with a guitar teacher that pretends to be an expert all while trying to smear innocent people. Why a person like Hyatt would behave as he has is anyone's guess but I think if he spent a little more time with his bible studies he may begin to feel overwhelming guilt for what he has done.

Statement analysis is a questionable technique even when done by the experts; the technique has absolutely no credibility when performed by guitar teachers. The truth has been available about Hyatt for some time now, yet Quennell's group continues to view Hyatt as an expert, completely ignoring reality.

Besides statement analysis, the guilters also thought they had a psychologist on board but it turns out they were duped once again. A woman named Ellie Ewing created a blog titled "Lies My Mother Told Me" in which she discussed the Amanda Knox case while representing herself as a psychologist with "many years of experience." She ironically referred to herself as "Miss Represented" on her blog while using her false credentials to provide analysis of Amanda's behavior in court.

The truth is Ewing had no clinical psychology experience and no credentials as a "psychologist", which requires an advanced degree at the time of her writing.

When Ewing's lies were exposed she quickly took her blog offline saying that she was no longer involved with the case. Unfortunately she was not outed until the appeal was coming to a close. Her fraudulent analysis was read by many over the past few years and was heavily promoted on TJMK. He proudly stated that his site provided the expert opinion of Ellie Ewing. To this day Quennell has never acknowledged that Ewing was a fraud even though the proof is now very clear.

I should not have been shocked by anything coming from Quennell's group but I must say that I was surprised to see Quennell embrace the views of an astrologer calling himself "Ergon."

Here are a couple of excerpts from Ergon's analysis featured on TJMK:

> *"The day of the murder saw widespread stressors on all their horoscopes which would lead to murder, detection, conviction and imprisonment. The Astrology even shows Raffaele's drug dependency and mental confusion on the night of the murder, the conflict between Amanda and Meredith, and the violence and rage that simmered just below the surface of Amanda Knox's psyche."*

> *"And the night of the murder, November 1, 2007, saw Saturn and Venus in the house of emotional excess, Uranus in the house of sudden death, and Jupiter/Pluto, in the sexual house, in an almost exact T-Square to each other. The close conjunction of Pluto to the Milky Way's Galactic Center shows the potency of this murder in attracting the public imagination, and also, the trigger for the murder."*

Why wasn't this brought up at trial? It all makes sense when you listen to Quennell's experts. Everyone knows that murders are more likely to occur when there is a close conjunction of Pluto to the Milky Way's Galactic Center! Of course we know this is all nonsense. Ergon's arrival to the guilter camp showed definitive proof that their group was completely void of any real expert opinion. Any experts that may have contributed early on are long gone, leaving Quennell and his followers with nothing more than delusional visions born from the stars.

The sad reality is that Quennell and Ganong have never relied on expert analysis or facts of any kind to keep their followers in line because their group is not fueled by truth, but rather by hate. The anger can be seen on their discussion board as many within the group often fight with each other causing an environment always on the verge of imploding, and eventually that is exactly what happened. Perugia Murder File had a civil war. Amazingly, it resulted in not one, but two PMFs. The original PMF was run by Peggy Ganong and a guy named Michael. When the website blew up, Ganong high jacked it throwing Michael to the curb. This led Michael to put a copy of the website on .net, leaving Ganong to run .org, all while refusing to discuss the details of their split. This of course often happens to hate groups over time. There is simply too much rage and they inevitably self destruct.

When witnessing how poorly the guilters treat each other it is really no surprise to see the group lashing out at others outside of their cult, focusing much of their rage on those who support Amanda and Raffaele. Unfortunately the attacks are not limited to anger filled rants on their forum. The group actively attempts to adversely affect the lives of those who disagree with their views.

Michael Krom is a professor at Leeds University in London. Meredith had attended Leeds University before going to Perugia to further her studies. Michael has been an active supporter of Amanda Knox and Raffaele Sollecito. His voice was heard in Italy when he was quoted by *Oggi* magazine.

A PMF poster named "Zorba" wrote a long letter to the Vice Chancellor and several other higher ups in Leeds University calling for disciplinary proceedings against Michael. Zorba's letter prompted the university secretary to write a short note to Michael stating that he was not speaking on behalf of the university but rather as a private individual. The secretary included the fact that professors at the university are free to express their views.

Michael Krom was not deterred by the failed attempt to adversely affect his employment and has never toned down his support. He has been in close contact with Raffaele Sollecito and has been active in helping Raffaele get a fresh start.

Michael Wiesner is a grade school teacher in Hawaii that found himself on the guilter radar when I posted a video online that he and his class created about the Amanda Knox case. Michael used the case as a case study in his classroom allowing his students to debate the issues and to design presentations detailing their views.

Shortly after I posted the video from Michael's class, The Anti-Knox group launched an all out attack on Michael and his school. Attempts were made to contact students in his class, the address of the school was posted online, and a photo of the school's principal was posted on TJMK.

Michael Wiesner has the full support of his employer but I made the decision to remove the video from the Injustice in Perugia blog because I felt it was wrong to ask the school to deal with the unnecessary distraction presented by the guilters.

Retired FBI Agent Steve Moore has been heavily targeted by the guilters for speaking on behalf of Amanda and Raffaele. Even worse, his family has come under attack. Steve's daughter had her Facebook account cloned in an attempt to impersonate her online. Letters were also sent to Steve's former employer in an attempt to interfere with his employment (more to come). One conversation on PMF regarding Steve Moore's past in infiltrating a white supremacist group highlighted just how ridiculous Peggy Ganong and her group can be. During that conversation, Ganong actually insinuated that Steve might be a white supremacist himself. When later questioned about her comment, she stood by her statement.

Journalist Candace Dempsey has to be one of the longest standing targets for the pro-guilt crowd. There is no doubt that she is disliked by the hate filled group because she was the first journalist to suggest that Amanda and Raffaele may be innocent. Anyone that has followed my involvement in this case over the past 2 years knows that I have great respect for Candace. My respect has nothing to do with the fact that Candace and I are on the same side of the debate; it comes from witnessing Candace's journalistic talent as well as her ability to remain professional no matter what her detractors throw her way.

Many guilters have attacked Candace but none more than the group's leader Peggy Ganong. Ganong has led a campaign of misinformation about Candace for nearly four years. Ganong often questions whether or not Candace is a journalist, insisting on calling her a blogger instead of a journalist and author, and often repeats lies about her career.

Ganong claims that Candace lied about her age on her Linked In account when in fact it was a typo. Candace's age was listed as 20 years younger than it actually was. Who would attempt to shave 20 years off their age? Ganong knows it was a typo but the truth is of little importance. Ganong's friend Andrea Vogt asked Candace about the Linked In error while they were both covering the case in Italy. There is no doubt that Vogt relayed the information about the typo back to Ganong.

Ganong often repeats her claim that Candace lied about working at the *Spokesman-Review* early in her career; when in fact Candace was a summer intern, working all the beats, including courts and police. The lie claim began when Monica Guzman of the Seattle PI interviewed Candace about her book deal in 2008. Guzman asked Candace where she got her training and she said, "At the *Spokesman-Review*." End of story. Peggy has been calling her a liar ever since. This despite the fact that the Spokesman-Review itself interviewed Candace for her book a year later and said she was a summer intern there.

Ganong made the erroneous claim that Candace was unemployed leading her to start a "food and travel" blog. This led many of Ganong's followers to begin calling Candace a "cook" instead of a journalist. The truth is that Candace was writing stories for *Puget Sound Business Journal* and other magazines at the time and was teaching an online class. The blog that Ganong refers to was something that Candace was doing just for fun. Even though Ganong claimed that no one read the blog, it was actually so popular that Candace was interviewed for Martha Stewart radio and was planning to write a book on the topic before securing the book deal with Penguin Books for Murder in Italy.

Ganong's verbal attacks on Candace have been relentless but the most egregious conduct against Candace came from Ganong's good friend Peter Quennell. Quennell made the ridiculous claim on his website that Candace was stalking the Kercher family. He made the claim based on a photograph of Candace taken in Italy while she was there reporting on the case. In the photo Candace can be seen walking behind Stephanie Kercher while she appears to be checking calls or texts on her cell phone.

Quennell posted large photos of Candace on TJMK and posted information about where she was staying in Italy. Candace was traveling alone leaving her vulnerable to hostility. Quennell made it very clear that his objective was to cause trouble for Candace while she was in Italy. Thankfully Candace was not harassed while in Italy but that does not diminish the disturbing nature of Quennell's attempts.

I did not become involved with the case until after the first trial had ended so I was not a target of the guilters when I first became vocal but I would not remain off of their radar for long. I have the philosophy that everything should be out in the open when it comes to information pertaining to the case. The truth has always been on our side so there is no reason to hide anything. I have taken the same approach when dealing with the guilter websites. I have made a conscience effort to make all information available to the public leaving them to decide who is credible.

In March 2011, I decided to write an article discussing the hate campaign raging on against Amanda Knox in the media that fueled the online hate campaign led by Peggy Ganong and Peter Quennell. This article would create an obsession with Bruce Fisher (me) on the guilter websites that continues to this day.

The original article was posted on Technorati.com. I

chose this web site because they seemed to garner good Google rankings. For a small time writer like me, nothing was more important than getting Google's attention in their search results. The article infuriated Peggy Ganong causing her to go on a manic campaign to have the article removed. She posted upwards of 100 comments on the article in a very short time frame. Every word in the article was truthful and backed by documentation but that was not enough to keep it online. Technorati removed the article because they host a "soapbox" environment and it is easier for them to avoid controversy. Keep in mind that the article was approved by Technorati's staff. They took the easy road on this one. If the article remained online, they would have had to deal with Ganong's relentless email and phone campaign. Ganong is known to flood email accounts with messages until she is heard. Technorati did not have a horse in the race so they simply removed themselves completely. It was unfortunate that Technorati was so easily influenced by a hate group but I understood their position.

Bruce Fisher became Peggy Ganong's obsession. Her avatar read "Bruce Fisher when will I see you" and it was obvious that I was on Ganong's mind day and night. Ganong and her friends also went to great lengths to find out who I was.

The attacks on me were nothing new as the guilters had shown similar obsessions with many others who supported Amanda Knox. I was just the latest one to have the honor. Ganong led an all out search for Bruce Fisher. After posting up several possibilities that all proved false, they were finally able to announce that they "found" me and that I had been "exposed." In reality PMF's "investigation" of me consisted of nothing more than someone trolling my Facebook account and obtaining information from a dishonest teen blogger who had attempted to use software to pull my IP address out of an email. Someone should have informed PMF that I was never in hiding, as it would have saved them a lot of time and effort.

I have always been available for anyone who wishes to speak with me; just send an email to injusticeinperugia@yahoo.com. The people searching for me have made no effort whatsoever to contact me. If I wanted information about someone who was readily available online, I would just ask that person.

PMF does not seem to realize that their obsession for Bruce Fisher proved what I knew all along. I have never worked for the PR firm Gogerty Marriott, I am not part of a super human public relations force, I am not a cameraman from Seattle, I am not a group of people using one name online, I am not Amanda's stepfather Chris Mellas, I am not any of the things they had claimed for over a year.

I will always be the person I said I was all along. I am just a guy that did what he could to help two innocent people who had been wronged by many. Injustice in Perugia is a grassroots organization that worked to correct an injustice. I am one person in an amazing group of selfless people that gathered to speak the truth. Injustice in Perugia brought actual experts together that analyzed the Amanda Knox case; working with real evidence. The truth was always clear for anyone willing to see it. Amanda Knox and Raffaele Sollecito were wrongfully convicted. Ganong and her friends refused to accept the truth, so as usual they decided to attack the messenger.

Ganong has repeatedly tried to smear me by making the baseless claim that articles written by me caused an anonymous Internet troll to post a threat against her on the website Perugia Shock. The senseless comment was removed by the website's owner Frank Sfarzo as are all comments of that nature. Injustice in Perugia has the same policy on its discussion board. I will not allow any hate speech or threats of violence of any kind to be posted on any website that I am associated with. Ganong and her friends have a different philosophy. Ganong claims that hateful comments on her website are protected by free speech. Ganong had no problem when her co-moderator Randy Jackson insinuated that he was stalking me by repeatedly detailing the location of my work, suggesting which restaurants that I may frequent nearby, and even stating the make and model of my car. Once again Ganong had no problem when a poster on her website named TomM repeatedly claimed to drive by my house in order to take pictures. Ganong was silent once again when I was threatened by her good friend Peter Quennell when he said this about me:

"I will bury him (I know where he is)"

Ganong has the philosophy that I needed to be "outed" so that I could "man up" for my accusations against her and her friends. She made these statements about me ignoring the fact that she is surrounded by anonymous posters spewing false information and hatred against Amanda Knox and anyone that supports her. Ganong's group has worked tirelessly to harm those that disagree with their views, all while hiding behind screen names. I wrote articles discussing Ganong and her followers because they attacked innocent people for years and the truth about their behavior needed to be told. Now that this case has come to a close I can only hope that the hatred will stop and reality will set in.

Ganong's creepy obsession with me was not the first sign that she had stalking tendencies. Ganong bragged about scoping out the Knox's home on PMF. When questioned about driving by the Knox home, Ganong claimed that she just happened to pass by the house on the way to another destination. Never mind the fact that she counted their shrubs to see just how much the Knox family may or may not spend on landscaping. I guess Ganong views that as normal behavior from someone that just happens to be passing by. Ganong likes to look at herself as a victim. In fact, she has accused me of libel for bringing her actions to light. Truth is an absolute defense against charges of libel. Everything I write is backed up by documentation. Ganong is trapped in her own words. It takes very little research to see that she is the aggressor, not the victim.

Besides being the aggressor Ganong appears to be a compulsive liar. She defends her lies by saying that she often posts non factual information simply to see what the reaction will be.

Ganong's most disturbing lie may very well have been a story she fabricated saying that a supporter of Amanda Knox harassed her and her family at a memorial service for one of her relatives. Here is an excerpt from PMF:

> *"I wasn't going to mention this, but a few weeks ago I attended a memorial service for someone to whom I am related by marriage (common-law marriage but it*

is a union that has lasted for 25 years and I consider my common law sister-in-law as family) and was surprised to see an FOA activist in attendance. This person did not know the deceased, though he knows and works for some people she knew, and was not invited. This person sat down two tables from me and seemed to be filming the whole time with a digital camera. I did not speak to this person. I got a call from my family members later in the evening, telling me that after I left, the FOA [Friends of Amanda] *enthusiast actually approached someone in my family, asked him if he knew about his relationship with me, and proceeded to ramble on about PMF, TJMK, Amanda Knox, etc. until my family member stopped him and said "this is neither the time nor the place for this conversation."*

"I felt bad for my brother and his wife: he had just lost a wonderful mother-in-law and she had just lost a wonderful mum. How anyone could approach them under the circumstances to spout incomprehensible acronyms and refer to a "relationship" with me is beyond my comprehension. And I still don't understand the presence of a camera. This event was not held in a church, but it was a memorial for someone who had died. When was the last time you or anyone saw someone snapping pictures or filming in such a context?"

Ganong was completely dishonest when she claimed that a FOA member harassed her and her family with a video camera at a memorial. The person she is referring to was hired by the family to photograph and take video. He is also not a member of FOA. He asked Ganong's brother one question about the case because he knew Ganong ran a website about the topic. I agree completely that this photographer (who wishes to not be named) should not have asked any questions at all because he was there to do a job but Ganong took one question from a photographer that is not FOA and spun an egregious lie. I did not mention the photographer by name because he does not want to get in trouble with his work. I have no interest in causing him problems with his job because he made the mistake of asking one question.

In another act of dishonesty, Ganong goes to great lengths to attempt to discredit the support that Amanda receives and she encourages her followers to do the same. One of her group's favorite tactics has been to exaggerate the scope of the PR firm hired by Amanda's parents. The truth is that Amanda's parents hired David Marriott to organize interviews with the press. They had every right to publicly defend their daughter. They did absolutely nothing wrong by hiring a firm to help them with a situation that was very new to them.

Ganong did not create the PR myth but she has campaigned heavily to keep it alive, often repeating the guilter catch phrase: "The PR Supertanker" when referring to any positive coverage for Amanda. The later chapters of this book detail the truth about the support that Amanda and Raffaele received.

Despite all the lies, Ganong's most despicable act has been to openly encourage her followers to attack Amanda Knox's family. Photos of the family are often posted on PMF with disparaging captions. One comment fuels the next with each poster trying to outdo the other. Amanda's parents are a constant focus of their attacks. Shortly before the end of the appeal, a poster named Emerald made this comment about Amanda's step father, Chris Mellas:

> *"It's past the point of utterly loathsome that Chris has moved away from his wife to be close to her grown daughter. Creepy. Makes me want to puke thinking about it."*

I was deeply offended by this comment but was not surprised to see that Emerald's statement was well received by her friends. Peggy Ganong is the chief moderator of PMF and she saw nothing wrong with the statement. In fact she posted shortly after Emerald's comment appeared and said nothing about it.

A PMF member named "Macport" made a photo collage of Amanda's sister Deanna crying at different stages of the trial simply to mock her. Other posters are critical of her outfits and cannot resist mocking her when she gives interviews. No matter what your opinion is of Amanda Knox, why attack her sister?

It is bad enough that the adults in Amanda's family are targeted but it is beyond repulsive to see both of Amanda's youngest sisters also being harassed. Photos of the two are posted on Ganong's website and members of the group, such as Julia Perez (Jools), a cyberstalking PMF member from Spain, have even made efforts to view their Facebook accounts. When questioned about this behavior the group claimed to be looking out for the children's safety. Two PMF members, Windfall and Earthling, suggested that the girls were "acting" when they showed emotion for their older sister. How does Peggy Ganong feel about innocent children being targeted on PMF? Of course Peggy Ganong continues to defend her website by claiming the posters have the right to express free speech.

I continue to be intrigued as to why PMF has continuously showed a disturbing obsession with sex in their daily conversation, attempting to paint Amanda's supporters as middle-aged men that only support Amanda because they are sexually attracted to her. Here are a few quotes from PMF:

> "All are middle-aged men driven by fantasies of recapturing lost youth, being a hero and carrying the damsel in distress off into the sunset."

> "those middle aged one hand typists who spend their sleepless nights imagining romantic interludes with Amanda."

> "seriously sick, pitifully perverted, lust aided attraction that some bored middle aged males with keyboards, have for a unanimously convicted, justly incarcerated young female"

Recently, this group suggested that Wikipedia founder Jimbo Wales became interested in the Amanda Knox case because he was looking to have sex with Amanda.

> "I don't see the pay-off in the end. Right now, Jimbo is on the verge of losing any sense of respect as a new media entrepreneur (lying about his checkuser results, for example) just for a chance to catch a peek of some tender young sex killer flesh."

> "Jimbo is precisely the profile of the aging Lothario

looking for access to tail through his powerful media connections. He isn't thinking with his correct head and everything he's proposed is straight out of the FOA manual."

"Somebody should give Jimbo a cold shower. He's really lathered up and ready for brunette sex killer action"

Ganong should have been ashamed to be part of that conversation, but as moderator of PMF she not only endorsed the dialogue but joined in with a zinger of her own:

"In all seriousness, what is it with these wiki guys and their wicks?"

Ganong's joke was pretty harmless compared to many of the comments that can be read on PMF, but her support helps to fuel the members in her group that had more serious obsessions. Ganong's good friend Peter Quennell appears to be the worst of the sexually obsessed in the Anti-Knox group. Many were shocked to hear what I discovered about the face of the Anti-Knox hate campaign in early 2011.

Anyone that has followed Injustice in Perugia knows that we have never shied away from criticizing those responsible for the wrongful convictions of Amanda Knox and Raffaele Sollecito. We have also been quick to call out people who provide misinformation and outright lies about the case, and also those who have gone out of their way to attack the families of Amanda Knox and her supporters. We have worked tirelessly to make sure that the truth about this case has been heard and we have done so without maliciously prying into the private lives of those who disagree with our position. No matter how vile our detractor's actions have been, we have never resorted to their reprehensible tactics in response.

IIP was faced with a tough decision when we uncovered information about Anti-Knox blogger Peter Quennell, owner and operator of TJMK. After a long discussion with the victim in this particular case, we decided together that Quennell's behavior could potentially harm others if it remained private. For this reason we made an exception to the rule when it came to releasing personal information because we felt Quennell's loyal following had the right to know about his conduct so they could take the proper precautions to protect themselves.

Peter Quennell's disturbing obsession with Meredith Kercher has long been a red flag suggesting that he most likely had deeper obsessions. Not only does Quennell post many photos of Meredith on TJMK, he also writes creepy articles about Meredith, a complete stranger, imagining what she would be doing if she was still alive. Quennell also takes interest in several other young murdered women. Photos of Natalie Holloway, Elizabeth Mandala, Laci Peterson, and Sonia Marra are posted. Quennell limits his coverage to young women. No male victims are discussed.

Quennell's infatuation with young women may seem harmless to the casual reader on TJMK, but unfortunately he crossed the line of human decency when his obsession led him to stalk a young woman in order to feed his desires. When the young woman refused his advances, Quennell tormented her, eventually demanding that she

121

pay him money to end the ordeal.

The young woman's personal information will not be revealed, as these details are not necessary to detail the reprehensible behavior exhibited by Quennell. For the sake of her privacy, I refer to the young woman as "Jane" and I describe her career as that of a "dancer."

Jane's nightmare began when Quennell attempted to work his way into her life by luring her into a business deal in which he would create a promotional website to help build her career. She was new to the United States and Quennell's offer sounded pretty good in the beginning. Quennell proceeded to create a website telling Jane that he was creating the website free of charge to show her the benefits of his promotional expertise.

Quennell was dishonest with Jane from the start when he led her to believe that he was an expert in website design. Up to that point Quennell had only presented a few websites online and they all used the same generic template. Besides TJMK, Quennell had designed a website for his condominium complex and another that highlighting dancers. All three websites have the exact same layout and could be created by anyone with minimal computer skills.

During the time that Quennell was creating the website, he offered Jane money on several occasions to help her through the tough times as she built her career. Jane told him repeatedly that her parents would help her financially. After uncomfortable pressure from Quennell, Jane accepted a cash gift from him to pay her rent. Quennell told her it was a gift that she did not have to pay back. From the tone of Quennell's future emails it was clear that he felt that the cash gift gave him a certain power over Jane.

Quennell convinced Jane and her friend to meet him in San Francisco to take photographs and video to enhance the website. This trip seemed to give Quennell a false sense that he was making progress with his quest to become closer to Jane.

Jane became increasingly alarmed when Quennell began suggesting that their business relationship should be a secret. She had no idea why anything should be a secret. She was also very uncomfortable with topics of a sexual nature that Quennell was sending in his emails. When reading the emails it is very clear that Quennell was looking for more than a business relationship. Quennell repeatedly mentions his own looks, suggests to Jane that it is perfectly normal if she wants to ask him questions about his sex life, and even goes as far as to let Jane know that he and his wife sleep in different beds.

When Quennell unveiled the new website, it included many personal details of Jane's life and she did not approve. Jane was shocked at the website Quennell had created and was also becoming further concerned (and was warned by at least one friend) that his interest in her was not solely business-related. He refused to cease communications with her when Jane suggested that they end their business relationship, and he appeared to her to be obsessed.

Quennell sent hundreds of emails to Jane, sometimes fifteen or more in a single day. The young woman that Quennell stalked and tried to extort money from is in her early 20's (Quennell is approximately three times her age). She had only been in the United States for a short period of time when Quennell invaded her life and was still in the process of learning the English language. She came to the United States pursuing career opportunities making her even more vulnerable to Quennell's claims that he could make her famous.

Here is a small sample of disturbing excerpts from Quennell's emails that caused Jane to quickly become uncomfortable with the "business" relationship between the two:

"But if I never meet your family and friends that is also just fine with me. If you think it best it remains a big secret, that could be a very good idea!"

"I should be back soon to looking way better than you have been seeing me! Your looking after yourself puts me to shame."

"I should tell you much more about myself. Women have always flocked to me for comfort and protection."

"Hope thought you should be eager by now to show that you trust me, not give me a hard time over small matters. She does kinda have a point. Please email me the address? I wont ever use it, never fear. She doesnt know about the phone number. Better we keep it that way."

"I dont much like hugging, but kissing on the cheek is something everybody does and all my women friends more or less insist on it. Hope gets a kiss on the cheek 10-20 times daily. You are the first woman ever to refuse and to even seem a bit horrified. And yet at the same time you shared a bed with Joan when you did not have to. If you are lesbian, I have no problem

*with lesbians - my best woman friend in UN is a
lesbian and I know many - and I will keep it a secret
forever if you want."*

*"You are a good chick. A very good chick. Tigress,
you could go a long way. Just love you in those boots
by the way."*

*"Also please ask me anything you like about my sex
life and my relations with women, that is only fair and
you too should be able to expect no surprises."*

*"For most of my life I was really very good looking
(like you)(and Hope) or so I was told like 5000 times!
So I was always being grabbed, and I hardly ever
really appreciated it."*

*"I should not have told you we have separate
bedrooms at home! At least without going on a while
longer. You'd be surprised how many men and women
especially if they are rich and have large homes
prefer to have their own space. It is not necessarily a
sign that they are short of sex or never spend the
night in one another's arms."*

*"By the way, you and I were alone together in a
room, and I was amused that you didnt even seem to
notice. You were very relaxed, in fact, and I really
liked and appreciated that. Remember where?"*
*"PS I'm looking way better too. Brown and really
quite fit.More of that to come."*

The emails from Quennell were disturbing to read and

will not be released in their entirety out of respect for Jane. The excerpts I have shown were approved by Jane and are more than enough to show how inappropriate Quennell's behavior was.

Jane wanted to end her business relationship with Quennell. She wanted the website taken offline and wanted the relentless emails to end. Quennell refused to comply and demanded money to remove the website. Quennell continued to send Jane hundreds of emails encouraging (pressuring) her to work with him. Quennell frequently attended events where Jane was performing, causing Jane to have an even greater fear for her safety. Jane built up the courage to respond to Quennell once again, asking him to take the website offline and suggested that they go their separate ways.

Jane's request caused Quennell to become even angrier. Quennell lashed out at Jane, threatening her career, her citizenship, and her future; looking for anything that would help him gain control. He refused to take the website offline and even demanded the money back that he gave her as a gift. The stress was too much for Jane and she decided to try and ignore his emails and accept the fact that the website that she did not approve of would remain online.

I first came in contact with Jane after I saw the website in question while browsing through the websites that Quennell had designed. I became suspicious about the website designed for Jane because I could not imagine that anyone would have approved of the unprofessional website that Quennell had created. After seeing Quennell's odd behavior on TJMK, I decided to contact Jane to see if she approved of the website. After Jane's initial shock that someone was contacting her to help her escape from her ongoing nightmare, she agreed to accept help to have the website created by Quennell taken offline. I put her in contact with a private investigator that helped her file a report with the authorities in her State. The detectives assigned to Jane's case immediately saw that Quennell was attempting to extort money from her by threatening to keep the website online indefinitely. Quennell was contacted by the authorities to take the website offline immediately and was told to have no contact with Jane or he would face arrest.

My involvement with this case has led me to come in contact with other women that have told me that they were also mistreated by Quennell. These contacts have chosen to stay silent for personal reasons. I encourage anyone that has been wronged by Quennell to come forward. Exposing the truth will help to prevent Quennell from mistreating others in the future. Quennell is the face of the hate campaign against Amanda Knox that continues to this day. If this information does not cause readers to pause and reevaluate what kind of person Quennell is and how credible his website is, nothing will.

Quennell's predictable reaction
The details of Quennell's behavior were first posted on the Injustice in Perugia blog. I also posted an article on Ground Report and All Voices, which are both citizen journalist websites. Needless to say, Quennell was not happy about the situation and scrambled to respond.

Unfortunately for him, his response posted on PMF was an outright lie:

> *"There is much missing from those emails on her side and nothing from what continued on Facebook. Several are fabricated and not written by me."*

It is laughable to think that any of the emails I presented were ever fabricated. Every email excerpt that I attributed to Peter Quennell was written by him and he very well knows this. He knows what he did was wrong. He complied with detectives when they told him to take the unauthorized website offline for that very reason. As far as the rest of Quennell's statement goes, I clearly stated that Quennell sent hundreds of emails to Jane. Jane's privacy is of great concern and the entire conversation was not necessary to show Quennell's reprehensible behavior. Nothing Jane said to Quennell warranted the emails she received in return.

As expected, a few of Quennell's loyal followers rushed to voice support. Most comments were nothing more than baseless attacks on me and completely ignored Quennell's behavior. Quennell's behavior was embarrassing and unacceptable, so I understood the need for his supporters to be in denial. However, to any reasonable person, Quennell's emails exposed him for what he really is. In the months that followed, Quennell's support base dwindled drastically.

I am rarely shocked by anything I read from Peggy Ganong, but I was actually a little surprised to see her response to the news about Quennell. Instead of distancing herself from Quennell's harassment of an innocent young woman, Ganong instead chose to blame and attack Quennell's victim, insinuating that she is hiding behind a pseudonym and acting immorally in order to run an online smear campaign against Quennell. (As an aside, Ganong should understand that it is in fact people like her who prevent people who have been victimized from speaking out in the first place. How can she then complain about anonymity?) Here is the exact quote Ganong used:

> *"Jane" and "Bruce" have violated one of the basic underlying rules of netiquette. Having done so, one apparently now wants to hide behind a "Jane Doe" moniker, while the other has always hidden, maintaining his status as a virtual non-entity who has been hired to run an online smear campaign as part of his job description. Whatever else happens, "Jane" has shown herself to be someone who has no qualms about taking someone's money and then not living up to her end of the moral agreement"*

The fact that this young woman wanted to protect her privacy needs no explanation. Ganong's comments regarding this young woman were shameful, but not surprising coming from her.

Caught in his own web of lies
Peter Quennell was once again shown to be a liar when he attempted to strong arm the Ground Report website into taking the article detailing his behavior offline.

Quennell contacted Ground Report to inform them that he was represented by a high-powered New York attorney. He has used this made up fact several times in the past in order to try to deter anyone from writing criticism about him. Quennell's lie was exposed when he attempted to namedrop this attorney in one of his many threatening email campaigns. Unfortunately for Quennell, this time the website he threatened legal action against actually took him seriously and had an attorney of their own. When Ground Report's attorney attempted to call the "opposing counsel" Quennell namedropped, lo and behold the namedropped attorney relayed that Quennell had misrepresented their relationship.

Quennell's actions make it obvious that he is a compulsive liar. In a lame attempt to explain his behavior on his website, he made the claim that he is actually the one trying to protect the young woman he has victimized. In his feeble attempt to defend his repulsive actions, he claimed that the young woman was tricked into revealing the emails between the two and she "rejects" me as much as he does. This could not be further from the truth and Quennell knows this; yet he chose to lie anyway, even when the truth was obvious. The most pathetic part of his lies is that even when trying to cover for himself, he could not help but disgustingly attack the young woman once again, even after his behavior had been exposed. His comment also suggested that he was still in contact with his victim which was untrue. Although, Quennell has emailed baseless threats that have all been ignored.

Once again, it is understandable why Quennell would lie to his ever shrinking group of followers. Everything I wrote about him is true, and thus his only option was to attempt to lie his way out of it. Quennell also suggested that he had a defamation lawsuit against me in the works. For those who do not know, Quennell has long claimed (even before the Ground Report fiasco) to have a high powered "attorney" that I need to fear because this "attorney" has taken down the mafia. I do not doubt that perhaps Peter Quennell has met a high powered attorney in his lifetime, but at the time of his threats it was glaringly obvious that he had no attorney representing him.

How do I know he had no attorney? Because if Quennell actually had an attorney who knew anything about defamation law, he would also know he had no case. Fortunately, Injustice in Perugia has several attorneys that have given me the tools to explain to him why I am not afraid of any of his baseless claims of defamation.

The truth is an absolute defense against a defamation claim. Everything I have ever written about Quennell is absolutely true, and Quennell knows this as well. Quennell also knows that were he foolish enough to file a lawsuit, he would be exposing himself to pretrial discovery, risking even further humiliation. Moreover, were Quennell to file a lawsuit, he would likely be deposed and face cross-examination by an experienced attorney. If entered into evidence, these depositions would all become part of the public record. If you have read Quennell's emails, it is obvious he would be his own worst witness. And, unlike his blog, where no one questions a word he says, he would be forced to answer questions under oath, something I imagine he is quite afraid of. Injustice in Perugia would be more than happy to have that opportunity.

I do know that Quennell has now hired an attorney (months after he claimed to have one), no not the high powered mafia busting guy, but an attorney none the less. IIP has been in contact with his "real" attorney and it seems that the only concern now is whether or not any lawsuits will be filed against Quennell for his reprehensible behavior.

I have personally been criticized a few times for how I handled the Quennell situation as some thought that Quennell's behavior should have remained private. Others claimed that the actions of our group made it look as if we were obsessed with Quennell. The truth is that Quennell was viciously attacking Amanda Knox and her followers with very little resistance before IIP took action. I believe it would have been foolish not to shine a light on his behavior. I included the information in this book because I believe IIP furthered its cause by exposing the Anti-Knox hate groups and highlighting Quennell's behavior was a significant part of that. By Investigating Quennell, IIP was not only able to help a young woman who was being harassed; we also silenced the loudest voice in the Anti-Knox hate campaign.

Unfortunately, there was a time when PMF/TJMK was respected by many casual readers as a source for information pertaining to the Amanda Knox case. After the first trial ended both Quennell and Ganong were interviewed by the media as if they were experts. This was before IIP exposed the truth about their reprehensible behavior. After the verdict came in on appeal declaring Amanda and Raffaele innocent, Quennell and Ganong were interviewed by no one. Once the truth was well known, the Anti-Knox groups were too toxic for even the yellow journalists to approach.

Injustice in Perugia will continue to monitor and scrutinize the actions of the Anti-Knox group leaders Quennell and Ganong along with their shrinking group of followers, whether it be connected to the Amanda Knox case or not, we refuse to simply turn the other cheek.

10

a strong showing of support

In the days following their arrest, much of the world thought that Amanda and Raffaele were guilty. As disturbing details of the case began to emerge suggesting that an injustice had occurred, support would slowly build for the two, eventually developing into a powerful force that was impossible to ignore. I have no doubt that Amanda and Raffaele's nightmare would have gone on far longer without the help of those who came forward to voice their opinion about the case.

The positive showing of support observed for Amanda and Raffaele has been carelessly misrepresented by the media, often suggesting that the support has been orchestrated by a PR firm at an estimated cost of one million dollars. It is time to put the lies about the "million dollar" PR campaign to rest. Amanda's parents hired a PR firm headed by David Marriott to organize interviews with the press, essentially working as a buffer between the family and relentless journalists. Amanda's family did absolutely nothing wrong by hiring a firm to help them with a situation that was very new to them. The agreement between Amanda's family and David Marriott has never been discussed publicly so the million dollar estimate parroted by the media is fabricated nonsense. There is also no truth to the suggestion that Marriott had a significant influence on the public support shown for Amanda and Raffaele.

The truth is the support for Amanda and Raffaele stemmed from many individual voices that stood up against an injustice. This support was spearheaded by a small group early on that would become known as "Friends of Amanda" (FOA). FOA was founded by filmmaker Thomas Wright of Seattle, Washington, consisting of only four people early on; Thomas Wright, Judge Michael Heavey, Attorney Anne Bremner, and Jim Lovering. The group expanded to five when Dr. Mark Waterbury officially joined after already completing extensive work independently.

Thomas Wright did most of his work behind the scenes, and from what I am told; he has done more for the cause than anyone will ever know. Mark Waterbury recently commented that a majority of the credit wrongly attributed to the PR firm, as constantly mentioned in the news, should have actually gone to Tom. Besides working with the media, Tom has also helped to coordinate the defense fund effort, as well as organizing a public forum titled "Amanda Knox: The case for innocence" at Seattle University in April 2011, featuring speakers Tom Wright, Candace Dempsey, Mark Waterbury, Steve Moore, and Paul Ciolino.

When FOA first got off the ground, they faced overwhelming opposition. The world was being fed lies and misinformation at record speed by the press eager for headlines but this would not deter FOA's efforts. Anne Bremner became the face for FOA, conducting hundreds of interviews on TV and radio, taking rapid fire questions on the case, setting the record straight one interview at a time.

Jim Lovering was given the colossal job of organizing the case files so that key elements could be properly presented to the public. Jim did a masterful job of completing this task, creating friendsofamanda.org along with many documents and PDF files that presented the evidence in a manner that was easy to understand. Besides everything that Jim has done in view of the public, much of his work has been done behind the scenes, providing information and advice to others that have contributed to the cause.

Jim was one of the first to speak out about the case on Candace Dempsey's blog on the Seattle Post-Intelligencer. Jim was part of a very small group that supported Amanda and Raffaele in the early days that he described as a "lonely, frustrating period." Thankfully, his words of support were read by Amanda's stepfather Chris Mellas. The two would eventually meet, with Jim agreeing to come on-board to help the cause. I cannot say enough about Jim Lovering, there is no one that has done more for Amanda and Raffaele than Jim has. I would have accomplished very little without Jim's guidance and support and I know that many others feel the same.

Judge Michael Heavey is a King County Superior Court Judge, in the state of Washington. He has been one of Amanda Knox's most outspoken supporters which has not come without a cost. Judge Heavey wrote three letters to the Italian council that regulates judges, in 2008, to ask that the case be moved out of Perugia and to protest leaks from the prosecutor, police and prison officials to the tabloid press:

> *"Amanda Knox is in grave danger of being convicted of the murder because of illegal and improper poisoning of public opinion and judicial opinion,"* Heavey wrote. *"I respectfully submit that the prosecutor's office, police and prison employees have made illegal and false statements ... These false reports have wrongfully poisoned the well of public opinion against Amanda."*

For his efforts, the Washington State Commission on Judicial Conduct decided to charge Judge Heavey with using the prestige of his office to advance the private interests of Amanda Knox. Judge Heavey was charged for having used court time, materials and employees to draw up those letters on official letterhead.

Judge Heavey could have signed off on a low-level sanction but decided he could not admit to wrongdoing because he acted according to his conscience and the demands of a higher moral authority.

Usually when a judge faces charges of misconduct, it is because he or she has gotten caught doing something that is morally wrong. Judge Heavey's situation is entirely different. He acted purely on the basis of compassion and his actions in no way advanced his personal interests. Judge Heavey is a decorated Vietnam veteran that showed courage and integrity by accepting personal risk in order to help two innocent people that had been wronged. Judge Heavey spoke out publicly about the charges made against him:

"Amanda Knox was a neighbor and a classmate of my daughter. The crux of the charge is that I lent the prestige of my office to advance the private interests of Amanda Knox. My letters were basically to speak out against the injustice of improper actions designed to prevent a fair and impartial trial. This is not advancing a private interest. It is addressing fundamental principles of due process and fairness. My actions were to serve the interests of justice. I hope that the Commission on Judicial Conduct will recognize that and acquit me of any violation. This is a pending matter and I will not make further comment at this time."

When it was all said and done, the state of Washington agreed that Judge Heavey did not "flagrantly or intentionally" violate the canons, and his actions harmed no one. Judge Heavey agreed his actions "negatively affected the integrity of and respect for" the bench and he was "admonished" for his actions.

Thankfully, Judge Heavey essentially received a slap on the hand for using official letterhead, allowing him to move forward with unwavering support for Amanda and Raffaele. Judge Heavey has given several powerful speeches regarding the case and played an integral role in drafting an open letter to President Obama urging the United States Government to take an interest in the case.

Dr. Mark Waterbury is a scientist and engineer that provided invaluable information to the public early on that was not being made available anywhere else. Mark's analysis of the DNA opened many eyes and helped to bring a great deal of support to the cause. Mark presented his analysis on his website Science Spheres and is also the author of "Monster of Perugia: The framing of Amanda Knox." It was Mark's website, along with Ray Turner's "Ridiculous Case" blog, and the FOA website, that deeply influenced my decision to become more involved.

Much like Judge Heavey, Mark's efforts also came with a cost, as his business was put on hold due to the thousands of hours he dedicated to the case. These sacrifices witnessed early on by the members of FOA laid the groundwork for the large support group that would build over time.

Friends of Amanda clearly led the charge for innocence in 2008-2009, with their acronym "FOA" becoming the brand most used by the media when describing anyone who voiced support for Amanda and Raffaele, but there was also significant support coming from independent sources not affiliated with FOA. One of the strongest voices was Candace Dempsey. Being a journalist, Candace did not sign up for any specific group or announce that she was taking sides. What Candace did was report the truth. With a majority of the media getting it wrong, it was Candace's courageous voice that protected journalistic integrity. This was an incredible act of support at a crucial time. I know I have already mentioned Candace in the media chapter but she deserves mention here as well. Those involved with this case in the beginning will never forget that Candace's blog was the battleground early on that would begin to build support for Amanda and Raffaele that never stopped growing until they were finally declared innocent.

Ray Turner is another name that was prominent early on and continues to be today. Ray blogs about the case on his blog The Ridiculous Case Against Amanda Knox and Raffaele Sollecito. His blog has been very critical of Prosecutor Giuliano Mignini, providing extensive information about Mignini, including his laundry list of lawsuits that he has thrown at people that have hurt his feelings, along with details of his pending conviction for abuse of office.

I first got to know Ray when I invited him into our private discussion group on Facebook. It was not long before he was offering me much needed advice such as "Yo, that website needs some pictures." Ray is another contributor that does a lot of work behind the scenes helping others with their projects and doing research. I have personally witnessed Ray's contributions, and I can honestly say that he has done invaluable work for the cause, never looking to take credit for his efforts. Ray and I have done a lot of work together on this case and I have a feeling we will find ourselves working together again in the future.

Chris Halkides, Associate Professor of chemistry and biochemistry at the University of North Carolina at Wilmington, has written a collection of articles on his blog A-View-From-Wilmington. His research has been phenomenal, often relating back to prior cases with similar situations, in order to support his position. Chris has been outspoken online regarding this case, always presenting his side of the argument in a very professional manner. I have appreciated the scientific information that Chris has provided throughout the case and I know many others share the same sentiment.

Andrew Lowery, a dedicated supporter from the beginning, knew that the truth about the case needed much greater attention in Italy, so he set out to create the website AmandaKnox.it. Andrew had Mark Waterbury's articles translated into Italian and also worked with Mark to create a series of videos highlighting the gross negligence of the police. Andrew would later update the Italian website with Steve Moore's articles, continuing to provide vital information to Italian readers.

On April 11, 2009, CBS aired the 48 hours Mystery: American Girl, Italian Nightmare, detailing the results of their 16 month investigation. As part of the investigation, CBS hired private investigator Paul Ciolino to take a closer look at the alleged evidence against Amanda and Raffaele. Ciolino traveled to Perugia, performed a thorough investigation, and determined that Amanda and Raffaele were clearly innocent. Ciolino described the case as "A railroad job from hell," a phrase that would be repeated many times throughout this ordeal. Ciolino's investigation led him to become an outspoken supporter of Amanda and Raffaele, often speaking to the public about the case throughout both trials.

Douglas Preston also appeared in the 48 hours documentary, declaring: "This is a case based on lies superstition and crazy conspiracy theories and that is it. It is a tragedy." Like Amanda, Douglas Preston knows firsthand how Giuliano Mignini and the Perugian authorities operate. Preston was interrogated by Mignini, accused of being an accessory to murder involving the Monster of Florence case. The case revolved around a series of murders that occurred in Italy during the 1970s and 80s. The perpetrator of the murders was given the name "Monster of Florence" by the press. Mignini dreamt up a ridiculous theory that the young couples were murdered so that their body parts could be used in rituals by satanic cults. Preston and his writing partner Mario Spezi thought Mignini's theory was ridiculous and were in the process of writing a book titled "Monster of Florence." Both Spezi and Preston were brutalized by Mignini in an effort to distract their writing efforts. Thankfully, Mignini was unsuccessful, as "The Monster of Florence" went on to become a bestselling book, soon to be depicted in a major motion picture starring George Clooney.

In late 2009, in an effort coordinated by FOA, a petition was drafted by Elizabeth Johnson, Ph.D., an independent forensics biology and DNA expert, and Greg Hampikian, Ph.D., director of the Idaho Innocence Project and professor in the Department of Biology at Boise State University. The petition was also signed by seven additional DNA experts. The petition concluded that the DNA testing results could have been obtained even if no crime had occurred, meaning that the DNA results did not constitute credible evidence linking Amanda and Raffaele to the crime.

Greg Hampikian did extensive research on the case, above and beyond his efforts with the petition, concluding early on that the science was faulty. Shortly after Amanda and Raffaele were declared innocent, Hampikian stated in a speech given at Boise State University, that when he first began his research, he had not intended on working on the case for three and a half years. Like many others, Hampikian was drawn to the case, and once involved there was no turning back until the injustice was corrected. Hampikian had this to say in conclusion:

> *"The original crime was only part of the suffering and victimization," Hampikian exclaimed. "These families that had accused children and convicted children also underwent tremendous suffering as well as the Kercher's who lost their daughter. The Kercher's were fed a story about three people when one of them only did it. And, now, where is their peace of mind? They were also robbed of what little peace that may up come from a clear trial. The lesson here is: do the science right."*

John Douglas is a former special agent with the FBI and is the most famous profiler of serial killers in the world. This should come as no surprise because he is the pioneer of criminal profiling. His life has been dedicated to bringing the most horrible criminals to justice making him the most well regarded voice in the field. Douglas was interviewed by Maxim magazine in 2011. In that interview he definitively states that Amanda Knox is innocent. Here is an excerpt from the January 2011 issue:

> *"Amanda is innocent—I'm convinced of it," says Douglas. "The Italian police completely contaminated the crime scene. Besides, behavior reflects personality, and there is nothing in Knox's past behavior to indicate she is a murderer."*

After the Verdict

Shortly after the verdict, Washington State Senator, Maria Cantwell, released a statement of concern regarding the verdict:

> *"I am saddened by the verdict and I have serious questions about the Italian justice system and whether anti-Americanism tainted this trial. The prosecution did not present enough evidence for an impartial jury to conclude beyond a reasonable doubt that Ms. Knox was guilty. Italian jurors were not sequestered and were allowed to view highly negative news coverage about Ms. Knox. Other flaws in the Italian justice system on display in this case included the harsh treatment of Ms. Knox following her arrest; negligent handling of evidence by investigators; and pending charges of misconduct against one of the prosecutors stemming from another murder trial."*

Unfortunately, little more was said by United States politicians, other than Secretary of State Hillary Clinton stating that her office was monitoring the situation. Thankfully Senator Cantwell's words of concern did not go unnoticed in Italy.

The Italy-USA Foundation, an association whose aim is to foster good relations and trade between the two countries listened to Cantwell's concerns and decided to conduct a well-being check on Amanda Knox.

Rocco Girlanda, the President of the Italy-USA Foundation, visited Amanda in prison and was surprised at what he found. It took only one visit for Rocco to realize that Amanda was not the cold hearted killer as portrayed by the prosecution, she was a kind and caring person who lost a friend on the night Meredith was murdered. Rocco's visit turned into many visits that led him to write a book, based on his prison conversations with Amanda, painting an overwhelmingly positive picture of Amanda as being absolutely incapable of committing murder.

Rocco also teamed up with 11 Italian politicians to file a petition to Italian Justice Minister Angelino Alfano, seeking a probe into the case, and the Italy-USA Foundation presented an open letter to Italian President Giorgio Napolitano highlighting their concerns. Rocco Girlanda has shown incredible support for Amanda Knox. Rocco was one of many that saw an injustice and worked to correct it. You will read about Rocco once again in the final chapter as his efforts to help Amanda never ceased until the day that she was safely home with her family.

Shortly after the verdict in December 2009, a grass roots organization was formed that would work diligently to further expand the support network for Amanda and Raffaele. This group was successful in bringing forward seasoned experts that helped greatly with public perception. This grass roots organization would become known as Injustice in Perugia.

11

a grassroots movement

I have been asked many times how I became involved with the Amanda Knox case. The truth is I do not know if I can pinpoint one specific detail that drew me in. I believe it was a culmination of many factors that just became too overwhelming for me to overlook.

I had followed the case throughout the first trial and I will admit that I was naive enough to believe that the court would get it right and find Amanda and Raffaele not guilty when the verdict was read in December 2009. I was listening to the radio at the time and I was shocked by the emotion I felt when I heard "guilty." I struggled to understand why I was affected so strongly by the verdict, as I had never been one to get overly emotional when it came to hardships suffered by strangers. It is not that I am cold hearted but I had always lived with the philosophy that we would spend every hour of our lives in a deep depression if we felt sorrow every time another human being felt pain or was faced with a tragedy.

So why was this case so different? Why was I unable to stop thinking about Amanda and Raffaele (two complete strangers), in the days following the verdict? These were questions that I could not answer on my own so I decided to research the case further. Of course, I did what any intelligent human being would do, I ran to Google and Facebook!

My Facebook search led me to the "Free Amanda Knox" page where I found many people discussing the case with a great deal of passion. This was to be expected of course because the verdicts were fresh on everyone's minds. I will admit that it took me quite a while to realize that the world now revolves around Facebook (at least that's what my kids think). In fact I found the Amanda Knox page shortly after creating my Facebook profile in December 2009, long after Facebook had achieved world dominance. Of course the Amanda Knox case had already been going on for 2 years, so needless to say, I was late to the fight.

My official decision to take an active role in the support of Amanda and Raffaele came on Christmas day 2009. Christmas is my favorite time of the year. My line of work keeps me away from home far more than I would like in the winter months, but nothing will ever keep me from home on Christmas day. I cherish that time with my family and absolutely love watching my children open their presents. So what could Christmas day with my family possibly have to do with this case?

On Christmas morning we all ran downstairs (meaning the kids dragged us out of bed and we stumbled down the stairs) to open presents. As I sat there watching wrapping paper being annihilated and boxes being held up high awaiting the flash of the camera (realizing once again that I was the luckiest man on the planet to have such an amazing family), I strangely could not stop thinking about Amanda and Raffaele. We have a teenage daughter and the thought of her being thrown into a similar nightmare somehow hit me at that moment, on Christmas morning, when nothing else has ever been able to distract me from the joy of that day. I sat there wondering who would help us if we were faced with that situation. What would happen to our family?

I never spoke of my feelings on Christmas day until I sat down to write this book as I still struggle to explain how I was drawn into this case and why it was able to change my way of thinking. I will say that I think the changes are positive and I now view the world a little differently than I did a few years ago.

We all know that Google and Facebook do not create experts on any given topic, but the internet is an incredible tool capable of bringing experts from around the world into one conversation, in turn providing vast amounts of information to educate average people like me.

When I began my research I realized that the case for innocence had already been documented online but the information was a bit scattered. I had a vision early on to bring all of the information together into one group in order to create one powerful voice for Amanda and Raffaele.

First I needed to become acquainted with those who had been fighting the battle for 2 years before I had even thought to help. Facebook was the fastest and easiest way to get in touch with all involved. Through Facebook I became acquainted with Jim Lovering, Mark Waterbury, Ray Turner, and Amanda's stepfather Chris Mellas. One of Amanda and Raffaele's core supporters, Eve Applebaum-Dominick, took the first major step in bringing everyone together when she created a private thread on Facebook that allowed us to discuss the case privately. This made it possible for the core group to discuss the case with our vital contacts, without fear of every word being twisted by the media.

If I had any doubt about the innocence of Amanda and Raffaele, it was eliminated after these friendships were established. From that point on, I was looking at case evidence in far greater detail than the limited information provided by sound bites heard on the nightly news. Unfortunately, this information was not being heard nearly enough by the general public.

In March 2010 I took my first significant step to help the cause when I founded Injustice in Perugia (IIP), an independent grassroots organization that would work to correct the injustice committed against Amanda Knox and Raffaele Sollecito. The organization grew rapidly after I launched the organization's website, InjusticeinPerugia.org.

As the support grew, IIP's core members were outgrowing the limited abilities of the private Facebook threads (due to the fact that Facebook limited the number of participants in each thread), leading us to attempt to move our discussion to a forum format instead, but that experiment was short lived. We all quickly found ourselves right back on Facebook, as it seemed to be a comfortable meeting place. To accommodate the group's expansion, the Facebook threads evolved into Facebook groups, giving us the ability to include more people in the discussion.

Utilizing Facebook to organize our discussions worked out very well but did pose security issues for some members of our group because Facebook was also the place they came to socialize with their friends and to keep in touch with family. The major concern was the fact that the Anti-Knox crowd is notorious for stalking Facebook pages, stealing photos and generally being pests. We had several discussions regarding privacy settings on our accounts as well as using caution when adding new friends. I was encouraged early on to take extra steps to protect my family from being harassed, with one suggestion being to change my name so that my children would not be located in a Facebook search. Removing the "c" from my last name did the trick. Now that Amanda and Raffaele are free and the hate groups have dwindled, I no longer feel the need to have this precaution in place. The actual spelling of my name is "Fischer." I chose to leave the name on this book the same as the first book simply to avoid confusion, but I plan on using the actual spelling for any future writing.

As the Facebook discussions continued to flourish, traffic to the IIP website also continued to increase. Our early success caused me to be even more eager to get the message out to an even larger audience. Many articles were being written about the case almost on a daily basis, and underneath those articles you could almost always find a comment section giving readers the ability to chime in. As I discussed in "Injustice in Perugia," those comment sections were often dominated by guilters, most specifically, Harry Rag. Several key supporters such as Joseph Bishop, Mary H, and Jim Lovering, were putting up a good fight but they needed far more support. IIP would do what we could to offer that support. In doing so, we also took the opportunity to advertise the IIP website driving in a great deal of traffic. Our job was to bring the truth to the public and this was a significant step forward.

In April 2010, IIP took another significant step forward when retired FBI Agent Steve Moore came aboard to offer his support and expertise. Steve's wife Michelle was posting messages on Facebook that her husband was a retired FBI Agent that believed in Amanda and Raffaele's innocence. A few members of IIP made me aware of her posts leading me to contact Michelle to find out more. Michelle was fantastic from the start, more than willing to help the cause. She encouraged me to contact her husband so that is exactly what I did. I spoke to Steve in April 2010 to ask him if he would like to become a contributor for IIP. He was more than willing to provide his expertise, writing a series of articles for the IIP website. Shortly after Steve joined IIP, Sarah Snyder (one of IIP's core members) arranged Steve's first TV interview in Seattle. This interview led to Steve making appearances on every major news network in America and several in the United Kingdom. He has been frequently interviewed about the case ever since, most recently in Perugia while attending the final court hearings. Thanks to Steve Moore, IIP's message has been heard worldwide.

I have never been a fan of Twitter but Ray Turner convinced me that IIP needed to be tweeting our message whether I understood the concept or not. So I set out to research Twitter finding out everything I could about the art of tweeting so that I could become a Twitter genius. No, I am just kidding, I did nothing of the sort. The reality is I posted a message on Facebook asking for volunteers to run the IIP Twitter page. Thankfully Patrick King and Sarah Snyder offered to take on the task. Kidding aside, Twitter has helped greatly to spread the message and to drive traffic to IIP. I truly appreciate the work done by Patrick and Sarah and I am sure I will eventually realize just how cool Twitter really is.

IIP was making serious progress and the influx of intelligent people was invigorating. The growth of IIP energized me to reach out for even more support, beyond that of which we were already receiving on Facebook and the IIP website. In May 2010 I created the IIP forum to reach out to those speaking independently online using other means, as well as to reach out to others that might be looking to join the discussion. The forum provides a meeting place for those who support the cause and want to learn more without having to deal with all the negativity online. I have been more than impressed with the intelligent thought provoking conversations that continue to take place. There are far too many people actively participating to single out individuals who have contributed to the forum, but I am hopeful that each and every member knows how much their participation has been appreciated.

Today the forum has over 1000 members and contains vast information about the case. The forum has also attracted several translators, who have helped out greatly, including translation of the Conti-Vecchiotti report, detailing the flawed DNA evidence in the case. Sarah Snyder has done an excellent job of moderating the forum and we are grateful to have Jason Leznek on board to help with technical support.

Many projects have been taken on by IIP to spread our message. The group has written letters to every member of Congress as well as to their local politicians. We have actively worked to counter negative comments online, as well as contacting news outlets, that often report misinformation, politely asking that corrections be made. We have done what we can to improve the Wikipedia article on the case, and have actively supported Italian journalist Frank Sfarzo who has faced constant pressure for the past four years. We have worked behind the scenes encouraging experts to come forward to help the defense as well as helping with translation when possible. We have also encouraged people to donate what they can to the defense funds and to write letters to Amanda and Raffaele.

In July 2010, IIP began collecting letters for Amanda and Raffaele on the Free Amanda Knox and Raffaele Sollecito Facebook cause page. The page is run by Jason Leznek (one of IIP's core members) and currently has nearly 2400 members. It has been an amazing experience hearing feedback from Amanda and Raffaele's family members regarding the impact of the letters, and supporters have also received many heartfelt letters in return from Amanda and Raffaele expressing their appreciation.

In September 2010 IIP introduced Forensic Engineer Ron Hendry. Ron completed an extensive analysis of the crime scene using photographs and video, providing invaluable information to IIP readers. Ron's job was to reconstruct the crime scene and I personally believe he did a fantastic job. I spent many hours working with Ron organizing the information he provided and doing everything possible to present gruesome photographs while being as respectful as possible to the victim. Jim Lovering took it one step further, developing a clear and concise analysis, meeting in person with Ron in Seattle to nail down the crucial bullet points. Ron's expertise led him to provide a presentation that would be suitable in court; when it was all said and done, I feel that Ron's analysis for IIP provides an excellent presentation for the general public.

In February 2011, my first book "Injustice in Perugia: a book detailing the wrongful conviction of Amanda Knox and Raffaele Sollecito", was released on Amazon.com as well as BarnesandNoble.com. I wrote the book as part of a continued effort to bring our message to a wider audience. The readership was not massive by any means but it did help to distribute the message, and also countered the lies and misinformation presented in Barbie Nadeau's book "Angel Face." It was a fulfilling experience to see my book on Amazon along with Candace Dempsey's "Murder in Italy" and Mark Waterbury's "Monster of Perugia." I will be forever grateful to Heather Coy for her help with editing. The book was a small contribution but one that I am happy to have accomplished.

In March 2011 I teamed up with my friend Ray Turner to begin writing a series of articles that we have posted on several citizen journalist websites. Ray and I researched many different sites looking for those that achieved high Google ranking. We found that All Voices and Ground Report best suited our needs.

In our articles, Ray and I have taken on the architects of the "Foxy Knoxy" myth, exposing the horrendous reporting of Andrea Vogt, Barbie Nadeau, and Nick Pisa. We have also stood up to the Anti-Knox hate group led by Peter Quennell and Peggy Ganong, helping to effectively diminish their efforts.

As expected, our articles did not go over well with the Anti-Knox group; causing them to find anything they possibly could to discredit our message. Unfortunately for them, our articles are fact based and well documented, so their attempts to discredit the content have been unsuccessful. The only thing they could ever come up with is the fact that our articles state that the author resides in New York, when in reality I live just outside of Chicago. Citizen journalist sites only allow one author per article. It should come as no surprise that I want to give Ray proper credit, because in reality, he has quite often been the co-author. Posting the articles from New York is my way of including Ray because that is where he resides.

Ray and I will continue without fail to expose anyone who finds it necessary to spew hatred at Amanda Knox and Raffaele Sollecito, or to promote lies about this case. Besides finding another avenue to present our message, I have found writing to be a very fulfilling experience and have learned quite a bit from Ray, who happens to be an excellent writer.

Many other supporters have written articles that have been featured on the IIP website as well as several citizen journalist sites, newspapers and magazines. Writers include; David Anderson, Joseph Bishop, Chris Halkides, Ron Hendry, Jason Leznek, Jim Lovering (a.k.a. Charlie Wilkes), Grace More, Karen Pruett, Michael Scadron, Nigel Scott, Sarah Snyder, Dr. Mark Waterbury, and Michael Wiesner. The combined effort has provided a constant flow of information online, helping to counter the small pack of yellow journalists that refuse to see the truth to this day.

I have highlighted the efforts of FOA and IIP but the truth is there has been an enormous amount of independent support coming from individuals that, although possibly influenced by the information we have provided, have chosen to not affiliate themselves with any particular group. This support has been crucial as well. A group of these supporters gather on the James Randi Educational Foundation website (JREF). The JREF discussion thread contains thousands of posts and has continued to grow considerably over the past couple of years. When I first signed up for the forum, the debate was pretty even, but as the truth has now become crystal clear, the ongoing discussion has become a good source of support for Amanda and Raffaele.

Injustice in Perugia has truly been a grassroots effort. There have been many individual contributions ranging from small projects like inspirational artwork and distributing bumper stickers, to larger projects such as organizing fundraisers. It is often the little things that have the biggest impact. For instance, a poem or video has the potential to bring in additional support and may even get the attention of an expert in the field or catch the eye of a journalist. Every contribution big or small has added to the overall success of the group. One example of the grassroots effort that has really stood out for me took place in a high school classroom in Honolulu Hawaii when a group of students put together a video highlighting what they had learned about the case during a class discussion.

Michael Wiesner, a psychology, philosophy, and history teacher at a private high school in Honolulu Hawaii, brought the Amanda Knox case to the attention of his students while teaching psychology. Michael has been teaching at the high school level for 28 years, and has been awarded teacher of the year. His current classes are Honors World Civ and International Baccalaureate 20th Century History, but he also taught psychology and philosophy for 25 years.

His specialty is critical analysis of sources and media literacy. According to Michael, students need to know how to recognize bias and evaluate sources. He says that one aspect of psychology concentrates on attribution theory - how easy it is to misunderstand other people, their actions, and intent. Michael knows better than most that in order to understand both history, and the actions of human beings, context is vital. It was Michael's many years of teaching on this subject that caused his peeked interest in the Amanda Knox case. Here's Michael's take on the case in a nutshell:

"Amanda was misunderstood because she did not conform to conventional behavior. Her actions were taken entirely out of context. Then the media frenzy that created the false persona of 'Foxy Knoxy', the misinterpretation of trivial actions like length of cell phone calls, and the fabrication of possible motives

*without a shred of evidence, led to a wrongful
conviction. This is how conspiracy theories develop.
Give meaning to meaningless events - and if you have
enough of them, people are easily fooled."*

Michael felt strongly that the Amanda Knox case was a
great way to teach critical thinking to his students,
leading him to use the case in his classroom as a means of
discussion. Michael was pleased to see his students take a
strong interest in the case:

*"Students relate to Amanda and Raffaele because
they could be any one of them. My students joined the
FB causes page, and then our school news team
wanted to do this video for their last broadcast. They
are following the case, and rooting for an acquittal."*

Michael Wiesner and his students are a perfect example
of the grassroots effort that grew to correct the injustice
committed against Amanda and Raffaele.

When I wrote "Injustice in Perugia" I included a section
in the back of the book thanking those who have
contributed to the cause. I am proud to say that the group
has now grown too large to single out every contributor.
Every single person involved has contributed and
everyone should feel proud of their accomplishments. I
feel extremely privileged to have played a small role in
the overall success of Injustice in Perugia. I will be
forever moved by witnessing such a dedicated group of
people coming forward to help two complete strangers,
looking for absolutely nothing in return.

When thinking about how to properly thank those who did so much to help, I initially began detailing some of the members contributions and reasons for becoming involved, but it quickly occurred to me that no one could tell their story better than they could, so I decided to ask for their input. I was once again impressed by the group when I received many heartfelt messages detailing their involvement.

12

words of support

Here is what some of Amanda and Raffaele's strongest supporters had to say regarding their motivation to get involved with this case. These heartfelt comments are listed in the order that I received them.

The comments have been subjected to minimal editing because I wanted this to be an opportunity for others to tell their story in their own words. I contemplated shortening some of the longer submissions but decided against it; concluding that readers could skip to the next chapter if they were not interested in reading every word. Some of the terminology used comes directly from our private Facebook group "AKRS." The name is a simply an acronym for Amanda Knox/Raffaele Sollecito.

As you will see, some of the comments were written before Amanda and Raffaele were declared innocent, as I collected these over an extended period of time.

Jeff Beverly

I was a latecomer to the cause of Amanda & Raffaele. Virginia is a long way from Seattle and there was no local interest or reporting that I heard of. I was oblivious to the situation while they languished in prison before and during the trial. I just happened to be walking by a TV that day in December, 2009 and caught a brief national news report that Amanda & Raffaele had been found guilty. That was the first time I saw a picture of Amanda and I was incredulous. She didn't look like a killer. She looked like a respectable and vulnerable young lady.

Contrary to what some would accuse us of, I don't support Amanda just because she is an attractive white American young woman. But I confess that did make me more skeptical of the court's finding. I think most people are more attracted to the causes of those with whom we share a racial, national and cultural identity. It brings it closer to home. "But for the grace of God, there is MY daughter/sister/cousin." And if it's a sin to feel sympathetic toward an attractive young woman, then mea culpa. I am only human.

My skepticism caused me to look closer at the case. I couldn't dismiss it unless I was convinced that she had been fairly tried and judged. I started reading and studying about the case. I wanted to hear both sides and decide for myself what was reasonable to believe. I wanted to see a rational explanation and motive, but I read about satanic rituals and sex games. I wanted to see if there was believable and certain evidence, but I read about cartwheels, buying underwear, and wearing a Beatles shirt to court. The more I read, the more certain I became that the ridiculous and irrelevant nonsense was a smokescreen for lies and a complete lack of proof. Within a few days, I became convinced that Amanda had been framed and railroaded; and by extension, that Raffaele Sollecito was innocent as well.

I tried to imagine how I would feel in that situation. I was overwhelmingly concerned for Amanda's physical, emotional, and spiritual wellbeing. I needed to reach out to others who shared my concern but didn't know how. Amanda's aunt, Janet Huff's Facebook profile turned up in a Google search. I recognized her name from Amanda's Defense Fund website and I joined Facebook so I could send her a message. She directed me to Amanda's Cause site, and there I found links to the other groups.

I am grateful to all the other supporters who have become like family to me. They are some of the finest people I've never met. I may not accomplish a great deal of importance in this life, but one thing I will always be proud of: I supported Amanda & Raffaele.

Alexander Jackson

I am Alexander Jackson. I am a lawyer and live in rural Manitoba, Canada, where I have practiced law for about 25 years. I have two former careers, as a musician and a banker. Building my career and my practice took a great deal of time and work, so other than the obligatory involvements with Amnesty International and other groups, mostly to put on my CV, most of my "compassionate work" was done for paying clients.

In very early December, 2009, something changed and changed forever... and it wasn't this case. I read the Reader's Digest condensed version of the book, "The Bite of the Mango," by Mariatu Kamara. Her story, and especially the triumph of the human spirit over the worst cruelty imaginable, hit me hard. I was still reeling from this when I happened to be watching the news of the verdict in Perugia. These things always hit me, because I really believe that it is a very sad thing when anyone must be punished. Some of the commentators spoke of an injustice and a wrongful conviction. This piqued my interest because, as a lawyer, I have seen this happen. I want to know why the legal system fails when it fails, so it can be made better. I care about the more philosophical and ethical aspects of my profession.

I researched the case. I read everything I could find and each new revelation, each new fact drove me to a steadfast belief that this was and is a terrible injustice. What is more, as I saw the tactics and behaviors of the Perugian authorities, I began to suspect this was no accident, but rather a deliberate persecution of innocent people. This combined with my still "raw" sense of compassion that arose from the story of Ms. Kamara, brought me to a point where I simply had to seek out others and do whatever I could to try to right this wrong. I realized that it was my duty, as a human being, to exercise the compassion I so recently found within myself, for the good of my fellows. I am sorry that I waited so long, both in this case and generally, to find my voice. Although I know my present capacity to help is limited by my health and professional obligations, I sincerely wish I had done more.

As time goes on, I see more and more what wonderful people both of you (Amanda and Raffaele) truly are. I also see clearly what wonderful families you have. I have faced attack from others who sought to destroy me and my family, although not to the degree you have suffered. I know what it means to have people who care and who are loyal in their support. I found I could no longer look away from the suffering of others. I know I can't help everyone, but I can help one or two people at a time and that is why I do what I do for justice in this case.

Amanda and Raffaele, I hope these words find you exonerated and released from prison, free to make your own plans and goals and to pursue your own lives. Because of distances, I have always doubted I would ever meet anyone else involved in this in person, -- you, your families or other supporters. Know, however, that in the same way as I would always help my son, I stand ready to help both of you in whatever way I can, if you ever wish to call upon that help. I wish you the most wonderful lives and the greatest happiness and success that it is possible for anyone to have.

David D. Kamanski, Esq. (aka Kevad)
I took a strong interest in the case early on after reading many online news stories in the days following the crime was discovered and continuing through January 2008 when they announced Raffaele's DNA was found on the bra clasp. At that time I was mostly saddened for Meredith Kercher and her family for the horrible loss that

had occurred, however I was already suspicious that the reporting seemed very biased and unclear as to what really happened. The story had caught my attention right away because of three factors in my past history. As a college student and then again as a law school graduate I had traveled to Italy & Europe for almost 3 months each time, and I stayed in Italy approximately a month on each occasion. I shared the desire at that same approximate time in my life of both Meredith and Amanda to learn about other cultures, and see how other people lived their lives outside my home area. Also, as a father of a teenage daughter who very much wanted to go to Europe and indicated she wanted to spend a year studying abroad, I felt it might be important as a parent to try and understand what had happened, so that someday proper guidance could be given to my daughter to help her avoid this type of nightmare. Finally, as a long time attorney I often find it helpful to learn about complex legal issues that are in the headlines, although the only other time I done so this intently was for about 6 months I followed the Natalie Hollaway tragedy right before my wife & daughter took a cruise of the Caribbean Islands that summer. However, over the next 22 months I only saw about 2 dozen news updates and perhaps a dozen online or TV video segments which did include Good Morning America, discussion of Amanda taking the stand in June of 2009, and a lot of discussion in November 2009 of the trial near ending. At that time I had understood that the prosecution lacked any real proof of guilt and that Amanda & Raffaele would be announced innocent.

On the day of the trial verdict I heard it would be announced at midnight Italian time, so I closed my office here in Orange, California and headed to my mother's home to watch CNN whom I assumed would have live coverage. When I turned on the news the verdict was just being announced live, and I was really quite stunned, and for the first time I felt very sad for Amanda and her family. My mom could tell I was upset, and asked me what was wrong, and I replied, "I think the court in Italy just made a huge mistake, and an American college girl was just wrongly convicted of murder."

Over the next few weeks I decided to review the online newspaper stories, going back to November of 2007, and going all the way through the trial. I then looked for web sites both pro guilty and against the verdict and learned of PMF, True Justice for Meredith, as well as the FOA and other pro Innocence sites. I wondered how I had such a strong feeling something was wrong, but thought perhaps I missed something that the court found compelling. As I noted all the websites, I read the current PMF discussion, saw many of their postings, and found their prior forum postings. As Christmas approached I was reading from May of 2008, through August 2008, and I continued to be baffled at the online positions of Michael, and Peggy as well as others, and each time I formulated some doubts about their facts, this guy kept posting almost exactly what I was thinking, like he was inside my head and saying; hey wait a second. That person's online name was Charlie Wilkes. As I woke up the day before Christmas 2009 I had pretty much decided that although there may be some facts I still don't fully know, I do know this; the prosecution had an obligation to prove guilt beyond a reasonable doubt, and they clearly did not do so. That day I went out to do last minute shopping at the Irvine Spectrum in Irvine, California. As I walked this nice outside Mall, everywhere I looked I saw couples that looked from behind to be short girl, with a taller guy, and they appeared to me to be just like Amanda & Raffaele. They were happy, they were holding hands or onto each other and they were free. I looked at my watch and it was near 3:00pm. I went back to my car several stories up in the parking structure and looked out on the pretty day at one of the main local sites present in Orange County, California facing east towards Italy called Saddleback Mountain, named because two peaks that look connected but are separate look just like a Saddle. I was really upset, very disturbed that an Italian Court could make such a huge mistake, and take away such a valuable gift of freedom. At exactly 3:00 pm, midnight in Italy and now Christmas day there, I took a picture of Saddleback, and being both angry and saddened, I said "Merry Christmas Amanda, I know you are innocent, I am so sorry you are locked up there in Italy, I am going to take the time, and do whatever I can to try and help!"

Several days later on about December 27, 2009 I wrote an e-mail to the FOA website, telling of my legal background, and my belief that the court in Italy had made a huge mistake, that they had not proven anything near the legal burden of proof, that I did not find the pro-guilt persons credible and that I supported efforts to free Amanda Knox. I received a reply a day or two later, and was really somewhat surprised that it was authored by none other than the one and only, Charlie Wilkes. I advised Charlie that I would spend the next few months as we waited for the Motivation report, reading EVERYTHING put out by True Justice for Meredith and PMF, and of course all the Pro-Amanda sites and I would get back in touch with him. In January of 2010 I saw a few Facebook sites, and joined along with a few sites Charlie told me to about over the next few months. He told me fairly soon a full web site would go up and soon Bruce Fisher did go up. Although I was not too active on all the Facebook accounts I joined, I did post with some regularity on Bruce's general blog. Eventually the motivation came out and I contacted Charlie for a copy and translation and the appeals which he sent, and then he advised of the AKRS website and had me join. I then was active on that forum as I read the motivation, and in May 0f 2010 I read the appeals. I saw many issues and also advised Charlie & Bruce of my belief that Rudy had been locked in the house given the broken front door key situation and also of the TMB issues. From the many links Charlie provided between April and June of 2010 I saw hundreds of police photos and videos, and learned of the many errors and mistakes they made. Eventually Bruce & I wrote summaries of the two Appeals and he posted them for all to read and see. At that point I was truly impressed with Raffaele & his attorneys with their appeal effort and truly understood just how innocent he was also. I then supported Steve Moore as he was fired from Pepperdine and continued to voice my thoughts on Bruce's Blog, Frank's blog, and more and more on Facebook. During the summer of 2010 it became clear just how many errors, mistakes and manipulations the cops, the prosecutors, their experts, the judges and the media had made. It became more of a certainty that not only had they failed to prove the burden of beyond a reasonable doubt, but that both Amanda & Raffaele were in fact 100% innocent. Accordingly, over the past year plus I have written and posted well over a thousand comments in support of Amanda & Raffaele's freedom. I have written to both, but primarily Amanda telling her of my hobby with digital cameras, and trips to Alaska, Japan and Palm Springs. I have written to Donald Trump, Frank many times, have helped with newspaper articles, read the independent experts report, and follow every hearing through the night. I remain very involved daily with the several Facebook sites, Frank's blog, Bruce's forum and add comments whenever possible to current news stories. I am so impressed with all the wonderful supports of both Amanda & Raffaele, as well as their families, and marvel at how we have shared so many great aspects online using now primarily Facebook so effectively. I have also met with several supporters for fabulous dinner and continue to offer my assistance in any way I can to help bring both Amanda & Raffaele back home safely. As an experienced attorney familiar with how courts function and how cases work, I see a lot of positive things now happening, and I remain always positive and hopeful that this major error in the Italian Judicial system, which so many have read about and know about, will be corrected, and Amanda & Raffaele will soon be released. As I stated on Christmas Eve, 2009, I won't stop until they are free!

Joan James
My husband and I were in Tuscany at the time of the murder. When we flew home to Portland, OR from Milano, the magazine kiosks were full of tabloid newspapers. I bought a British paper and the more I read, the more bizarre it sounded...especially a young woman from Seattle...that's granola country (just like Portland)...anyway, it just didn't sound right. After I got home I followed the case and the more I read, the less I believed. I really felt a connection to Amanda...my

background is similar. It's not that I'm so smart and realized right away that she & Raf were innocent...it's just that it didn't ring true and my stomach turned over when I read what she was going through. Like her family, I believed she would be exonerated and they both would be released. I was shocked at the verdict and that's when I really began to get involved and started posting comments, writing letters and finding groups like Injustice in Perugia. I read Candace's book and also forced myself to get through Nadeau's. Obviously, Candace's book was objective, balanced and gave a clear picture of the situation. I won't comment here on Ms Barbie...my feelings about her are pretty well known as I post them wherever I can find a place.

Candace Dempsey came to PDX and had a book signing at one of our local book stores. My husband and I attended and I had the opportunity to chat briefly with her which only made me more certain that we were witnessing a modern day witch hunt. I had also read "The Monster of Florence"...just by chance I picked it up thinking it was about a medieval serial killer (lol). I was in a hurry and didn't read the fly leaf. As it turned out, I was riveted and then when I heard that Mignini, the psycho prosecutor in the book was also the prosecutor in Amanda's case, I was stunned.

I got involved for a variety of reasons...as I said; I felt a connection to Amanda as a fellow Pacific Northwesterner. I admired how hard she worked to get to Italy, the goals she had, her intensity and sincerity, her desire to mingle with Italians rather than stay safely with Americans, her slightly retro "hippy" persona (I'm a product of the hippy era)...just all the admirable qualities I found in her as well as those I found in Raf. One thing I remember vividly...the first time I saw the pic of them together outside the cottage. So many of the descriptions that came out of Italy said they were making out, smiling, ignoring the horror of what had happened inside...before we even read those descriptions and just saw the pic, my husband and I both felt that she looked totally traumatized and Raf was comforting her. I think that symbolizes the many differences in perspective (which I know were mostly created by the worldwide tabloid media) which have followed this case from the beginning.

I'd like to take this opportunity to tell you how much I admire what you have done for these kids. Your book was amazing, I read everything you write wherever I can find it and I just hope all the time and effort you and so many others have put into this will bear fruit in September.

S. Michael Scadron

I'll try to be brief. I'm a bit of a Johnny Come Lately compared to many on AKRS. This case first grabbed my attention around the time of the verdict in Dec. 2009, so I missed out on the media frenzy of 2007-08. I was taken in by interviews given by Curt & Edda and various accounts at the time (Timothy Egan's blogs in the *NY Times* and the Afterword to *Monster of Florence*), I found that the case made no sense. The more I read the less sense it made and the whole scenario seemed heart wrenching.

Until my retirement in 2006, I'd been a trial attorney at the Department of Justice for over 30 years. As I've said elsewhere, logic is the crutch that carries me through each day, common sense my failsafe. And when senseless and cruel stuff like this happens I get upset. I came of age during the 1960's, a time of great change. My sense of justice, or outrage at injustice, was formed, in part, by images on our TV in the corner of our living room in our Manhattan apartment, showing protesters in Birmingham, Ala. beaten with clubs and dispersed with water hoses and dogs. I worked for 6 yrs at DOJ in the Civil Rights Division's Voting Rights Section before moving to the Torts Branch (Civil Div.). At Torts my cases focused, in large part, on the reliability of scientific evidence and I conducted a number of *Daubert* hearings (see Mark Waterbury's book) trying to preclude the use of junk science in the courtroom. I witnessed how easily a judge -- not to mention a jury -- can be swayed by the lingo of science even where the scientific methodology is flawed.

I sent Amanda some books in Jan. 2010 with a short note and she responded. I continued to send letters to her in prison encouraging her to write her stories (I have, myself, taken up creative writing in retirement -- personal essays, short fiction and journalistic pieces). I joined FB so I could post comments on the *Free Amanda Knox* page and posted comments on the IIP pre-Forum discussion page. Eventually Joseph Bishop invited me into AKRS. (I don't mind telling you that it took me several weeks to figure out what AKRS stands for). I became obsessed with the case and continued with email messages to Amanda & Raffaele and wrote various articles, including the one published in the *Christian Science Monitor*.

When I first contacted Amanda I told her about certain physical challenges I've endured, a saga I also shared with Raffaele, and don't mind sharing with the group. You might call it my "kindred spirit" card. It's not so personal actually, as I'm working on a memoir I hope to publish which I call *Two Mountains,* focusing on a neurologic illness that struck me soon after my wife, Terri, and I summited Kilimanjaro, rendering me temporarily quadriplegic. For about 3 years I was bound to a motorized wheelchair unable to lift myself out of it without assistance. I was a 7- minute miler and avid hiker so, like Amanda and Raf, my world was turned upside down. I worked hard with physical therapists and eventually regained the ability to walk. My mantra which I repeat in some of my messages to Amanda and Raf is "We survive what comes over us, what finds us out of nowhere." (A 500 word essay distilled from a chapter in my book which I also titled *Two Mountains* is in the current issue of bethesdamagazine.com).

Timothy Jake Holmes
How did I get involved with the FOAkrs Majestic-50? Initially I accepted Amanda's guilt without question. They said they had a ton of proof; prints, blood evidence, footprints in blood. A CONFESSION. Clearly an American girl gone wild. However, as Amanda's trial ground on it became apparent that the whole sordid story woven by the Perugian authorities and merrily perpetuated by the British tabloid press was based on innuendo, speculation and mean spirited gossip rather than any sort of real evidence, and I became really

outraged. Every day I read in the paper of wars and famine, plagues, crumbling economies, spiraling deficits, Wall Street bail outs, a million things that I could do little or nothing to change. I, as an individual, can't save the world, and it frustrates the crap out of me. But with this case, about a local girl, I saw that maybe I COULD help. So I went searching online for like minded people and found InjusticeInPerugia.org. I've never really enjoyed discussing true crime and this was no who-dunnit, but I was struck by a statement Bruce Fisher made in his introduction to the site. "This isn't a place for debate. The time for discussion is over. Amanda is innocent. It's time to act." That kind of bold statement suited me fine and I signed up. Then one day I got a message from a guy I didn't know. He'd read some of my writing on IIP and thought I might be interested in a VERY AMBITIOUS plan he had to assail a very entrenched and well fortified Guilter position and sent me a link to AKRS PD. I anticipated that the group was probably made up of a handful of Pro-Amanda bloggers that just wanted some private talking space. When I read the list of members, which includes a who's who of the biggest movers and shakers in the grassroots pro-Knox movement, a light bulb came on over my head and I was both honored and flattered to have been invited there. Now it would take the Jaws of Life to pry me out of the group.

Shirley Anne Mather
How did I become interested in your Case? Well, I arrived here by happenstance, just like most of the other supporters. I have believed in your innocence from Day One and followed the initial trial very closely indeed. I felt that the pieces just didn't fit at all. It just didn't make

sense. I knew you were both innocent people and had nothing to do with the crime. When the Guilty Verdict was announced in Dec. 2009, my heart sank and my eyes filled with tears. I was absolutely heartbroken for you and your families.

This was a most serious miscarriage of justice and I just couldn't stop thinking about it and wanted to try and help in some way. I searched Facebook and came across "The Free Amanda Group". I joined immediately and later became a member of many of the other Amanda and Raffaele Support Groups on Facebook. I have been an Administrator on "The Free Raffaele" Site for about eighteen months and have been on there almost every day.

I have read several books, written about the case and I have also read the information over at InjusticeinPerugia, along with many other articles.

Your plight affected me in a very profound way and not a day goes by when I don't think about you. I have written to you both on many occasions and hope that my letters have helped you in some small way. I have prayed for freedom and exoneration for you both each and every day.

I was overjoyed when the conviction was overturned on Oct. 3rd 2011. So happy and relieved for you both. The nightmare was over - you were free. At last, you had your lives back.

You will always have a very special place in my heart. I love you both. God bless you, Amanda Knox and Raffaele Sollecito - I WILL NEVER FORGET YOU! You are an inspiration. Good luck, my friends. Sending you both much loving kindness. I hope to meet you both one day.

Eve Applebaum-Dominick

I became interested in Amanda Knox and Raffaele Sollecito back in 2007 when I saw, "an American girl was arrested in Perugia, Italy", along with her then Italian boyfriend, who happened to look like Harry Potter (a story and character I have always felt a strong affinity towards). Having studied in Italy at the same age as Amanda, 20+ years ago, and having lived, loved, marrying a handsome & kind Florentine young man as well as growing my butterfly wings there in Italy, I felt a deep personal connection to this case. Immediately, looking at the news on TV back in Nov 2007, my thought was, "both Amanda and Raffaele strike me as innocent". The moment I saw their faces on TV I knew, "no way; something is amiss here. Neither this girl nor this boy have killed anyone!". Soon after that news was released though, I had believed they had been set free, only to find out much later by a friend on the Italian Police Force, they were not at all free, but instead, in August 2009, were still incarcerated. At that point, I began to immerse myself in this case.

I was outraged these young people were, what I perceived, wrongfully accused. As I mentioned, having been an exchange student in Florence, Italy at the same tender age as Amanda, and having a history as a young naive American girl arriving in Italy from a safe place in my home with great family, lots of friends and security, right away I saw my young-self in Amanda Knox, and so did my Italian Police friend, hence he kept sending me info about her and Raffaele asking my thoughts.

I began reading, eating, sleeping and breathing Amanda Knox & Raffaele Sollecito. I was consumed with the idea they were STILL imprisoned. To me, it made NO sense what-so-ever. Everything I was reading, the video's I was watching and all of the circumstances clearly pointed to innocence; not to mention they had not even been tried yet and were being held without bail. Sometime in late Fall of 2009 a supporter named Jodie Leah and I started talking privately and she put me in touch with Raffaele's sister Vanessa Sollecito. Since Jan 3, 2010, nearly 2 years ago, Vanessa and I have emailed, telephoned, texted, IM-Skyped and/or video-Skyped every week, some weeks almost every day. The beauty of technology, where a person can sit face-to-face with another person, see and express WITH that person the myriad of emotions that run the gamut of human capacity, from mere facial expressions, to smiles, tensions, laughter and tears, has given us a great gift amidst this tragedy.

Right away in talking to Vanessa I came to learn she really wanted to create a website, similar to the beautiful one Jim Lovering created for Amanda, for Raffaele. I contacted Mark Waterbury first after seeing the Italian website featuring his work which I found wonderful and that explained clearly the forensics of the case and reasons the Science and facts of the case plainly pointed to innocence. Mark put me touch with Amanda's step-father Chris Mellas, Andrew Lowrey & Tom Wright who in turn put us in touch with Jim Lovering. Jim, what a wonderful man. The following months Jim was incredibly patient while he created the website Vanessa wanted to build for her beloved brother Raffaele. He created and re-created each aspect of the site as closely to her specifications as he could. Vanessa provided art idea's, photo's and collected testimonial's from all the friends and family who love Raffaele. It was a true labor of affection and when we finally completed the web site, I began the process of translating it to English. During that time, I got to know Raffaele on a deep level, having read the biography he wrote and the many beautiful things everyone wrote about him.

I tried to be available for translations whenever called upon after that. There was so much to do and I was helping a supporter named Jo also translate the Micheli report when it came out. When Bruce started his web site, sometimes I would help with translations, but it became overwhelming and I believe Bruce found someone to help him, which I was glad about.

In the Spring of 2010 an Italian TV segment aired in Italy called, "Altra del Meta del Crimine" on the channel "La7". It was a real-life Crime show and in this segment it followed an American woman living and writing in Italy named, Andrea Vogt, a self-professed guilter, and an Italian Forensic Scientist named Lt. Col. Luciano Garofano. They walked through the case on a very superficial level, visiting with some of the attorney's in the case as well as basically giving a duplicitous view to the audience by inferring credibility to, Low Copy Number DNA findings. (Later in the appeals, thanks to the independent experts, the truth of the DNA facts and the mishandling of it was exposed and anyone watching this show would know what a farce it was.) After seeing this show Jim and I spoke about it and he was very supportive of my trying to create another segment countering that one either in Italy (or in the US). By the end of the summer I had spoken to some producers in Italy and having a background in film production I was actually raising interest. However, the idea was cut-off because some of the defending attorney's felt it could interfere with the upcoming appeals. The defending attorney's did magnificently in the appeals and we all could not have been more thrilled by Amanda and Raffaele's exoneration.

Since Raffaele & Amanda's release, Raffaele and I have also been growing a friendship through the same resource used with Vanessa. "Skype" has been a huge part of "helping" an important healing process for Raffaele and knowing how amazing Vanessa is, and now, Raffaele too, I truly think the "Skype" people should know how significant and important their technology has been through this ordeal and their support in the healing process. No man is an Island and true friends come in all different packages, even through ones far away and unexpectedly outside the traditional box thought of as a conventional demographic.

In the summer of 2010, my husband and I went to Italy to visit my long-time friends and see my cousin and his wife and children who live there for more than 20 years. During that trip we were also honored guests of Vanessa in her home in Rome. By that point as she and I had deepened our friendship and trust we both agreed to have found a strong bond. I am so fortunate to know Vanessa, Raffaele (as well as Doctor Sollecito and his wife, Mara too) who are extraordinarily kind and lovely people.

All the reasons I felt compelled to help Amanda and Raffaele and do whatever I could, from the smallest thing to as big as was in my power, are justified through knowing of Amanda & Raffaele's innocence and from recognizing that they and their families are such exceptional people.

For me, having been so intensely involved in a

support team that grew from a few like-minded people in a Facebook private message box, to a group of 50+ people, has been an incredible experience. I've been fortunate to be a part of and to watch a grass roots group develop to a strong and united force. ALL for free. None of us made a dime. Contrary to what "guilters" think, THAT is a fact. I've also grown to know who Amanda Knox and her family members are, particularly Chris Mellas (and through him...Amanda's mother Edda as well); I feel I've been so fortunate to learn they are the most incredibly admirable, kind, brave, compassionate and dignified people. There is so much more I want and can say about Amanda and Raffaele and their families and what has happened to them; the fantastic adjectives, the elated feelings and the earnest thoughts seem to be like a run-on sentence that never ends in my mind. I could never imagine how it was for Amanda; to have her housemate murdered and then to be accused of it by people of the judicial system, people we learn are the people we should trust, the people who, we learned are the ones who make the right decisions and judgments in life. I can imagine the terror and confusion. For Raffaele too, the situation must have been so bewildering and completely horrifying. It breaks my heart to think of them both in that situation, while in the midst of the greatest feeling on earth, what humans live for... "love", experiencing a connection to another (young) person, with the sparkling stars in the eyes and the tenderness of passion and endorphins racing...for that to be ripped away and to be abused physically and emotionally and to be isolated from one moment to the next, is incomprehensible and cruel. For this, I felt compelled to do whatever I could to help soothe this trauma. I was motivated to help whoever I could that is either them or close to them. After experiencing 9-11 down the street from my home and knowing people I care about were there, I swore I would always become proactively involved in "crises" where I could. I became a Social Worker for that reason after 9-11 and I found here in this case, I could "help". Along with the many others in the support group, ALL incredibly outstanding people who have dedicated so much time and effort in this quest to support these two innocent people, I have personally grown as a human being and have been lucky enough to have acquired a great deal of good friends.

Though I am not a religious person, I must confess I believe, "everything for a reason" and like monks who are imprisoned for worshipping Buddha and when released continue their quest in peace and advocacy; Amanda & Raffaele will soon understand "why" and continue their lives with great purpose. As I get to know Raffaele and the friendship flourishes as much as it has with my dear friend Vanessa, and as we exchange stories, feelings, experiences, thoughts and ideas, I trust I understand him (and he me, as he's an interesting and interested young man) and I see clearly how Raffaele and Amanda could have been so drawn to one another.

The most important thing is my thoughts, instincts and feelings about these two honorable people has been validated. What I always knew in my heart, I now know deep in my flesh, bones, and soul. That Raffaele and Amanda have been worth this effort and sometimes fight to be able to witness and experience their freedom.

My comrades in this group of supporters are certainly all tremendous and impressive people, "heroes", whose sustaining devotion of 2 remarkable young people has come to fruition. We all knew Amanda and Raffaele are nothing what some of the media created. An ugly meme was created to serve a very greedy and careless few. We have also learned that the Media is a very tricky machine that can help report and spread important news, but also, alas, has the potential to create damaging lies.

I just want to conclude how sad I am about Meredith Kercher's murder. I wish the memory of her beautiful life was not doubly marred by 2 innocent people accused of her death in such a terrible hateful crime they COULD never have done. I feel for the Kercher family pain. I hope they can one day heal and relish in the memories of a short life lived to the fullest.

Karen Pruett

Amanda's dad Curt is a family friend and I learned of her arrest on November 8, 2007. It was confusing and at first I wondered what she had fallen into. Vashon Island, where her dad grew up and her grandparents still reside, was rife with gossip; normal for such a small town. I did not personally know any of the family, but my in-laws knew all of them. As details spilled out in the press we learned that much of it was lies and that Amanda had been railroaded, she was 100% innocent of Meredith's murder. I never doubted her innocence after mid-December 2007 and that knowledge made the debacle all the more painful.

My anguish and tears began in earnest by January 2008; I knew it was very bad and that she was in a lot of trouble. My heart broke for Curt and Cassandra and the rest of her family, but we could only stand on the sidelines watching and waiting. The media never came to

Vashon, we were protecting Curt's parents by keeping a low profile, but the fear of invasion was there as we watched what was happening to him in Seattle. It was surreal.

The guilty verdict in December 2009 was devastating. Seething anger; that is the only way I can describe how we all felt.

By August 2010, I finally met Curt and Cassandra at a party and realized in a brief conversation that chunks of information were missing because of the slanted media and informational blackout on Vashon. The next day I decided to buck family opinion and clandestinely began to research the case. As a long-time genealogist I applied my research skills and eventually found the police videos on YouTube and the Massei Motivation. I ignored all of the media outlets, considering them prejudiced. One hundred pages into the Massei, I knew exactly how Amanda had been railroaded and was furiously outraged.

After finding Mark Waterbury's analysis of the Massei, I followed the trail to Injustice in Perugia and our Facebook pages.

Embarrassed that there were fundraisers all over except Vashon, I screwed up my courage and asked Curt if I could do one. That opened the door to meeting his entire family, and Edda's. I was completely taken by their warmth and giving natures, that they fully supported Raffaele and his family and that they were filled with sympathy for Meredith and her family. I was incredibly touched by their generosity and by all of the ways our lives had intersected over the years. Amanda was our catalyst and it clear that life will surprise you with amazing coincidences.

After Vashon's benefit it was clear that Islanders hungered for information about Amanda and I began to write what I thought would be a couple of articles for the Vashon Loop, well I recently found out that I am a columnist! LOL!! My articles have put the entire Island solidly behind Amanda, Curt and his family and I don't care if anyone else reads them; I do this for my friends. Recently I learned that Curt's parents find out more from my column that they do from Curt and look forward to reading it, I am humbled and happy! But even my column was supported by all of my advocacy friends, your willingness to proof read and give suggestions has given me much needed confidence.

Because of Injustice in Perugia and all of the good people who are connected there, I found myself in a unique position to get succinct and correct information to share with Island neighbors.

I see the hand of God on our shoulders, gently guiding us, setting each of us to a task and each of you who have helped my friends, have helped me. You have been a balm to a frustrated and troubled soul. We will soldier on together to the end and I know I am no longer alone. When Our Kids are home and the dust has settled I will always remember each of you and wish you well wherever life takes you. I am proud to have known everyone of you good people.

That you have been there for my friends means everything to me. We are all in your debt! Thank You Always!!

Michael Krom
Why did I get involved in trying to help Raffaele and Amanda get justice: I visited Perugia in August 2007

attending a Geosciences' conference. Then in November I saw the news that Meredith Kercher a student from Leeds University, my university, had been murdered in the Italian town I had just visited. Over the next couple of weeks, the students who were on campus set up an impromptu shrine to Meredith in the centre of the university. One could not help but feel involved.

Like everyone else I then followed the news and the announcement that the police in Perugia had solved the case. Again, since I follow the news, and this was big news, I followed Amanda and Raffaele's detention and the exchange of Patrick for Guede. At that point it did seem that in arresting Rudy, they had caught a person involved in the crime. However at that stage I did not know enough to feel uncomfortable about what was being done to Amanda and Raffaele.

Rudy was convicted which seemed to be correct. The trial of Amanda and Raffaele was covered but not in great detail, the usual media sound bites. Then came the verdict and at that stage my 'gut' feelings were already aroused and when I heard they had been sentenced to 26/25 years I said out loud to my son who had found out the news on his Blackberry, 'That cannot be right!' His comment back was 'I thought you were supposed to be on the side of Meredith.'

From then on a started to search the internet for more information and found IIP. The more I read the more I thought that a grave injustice had occurred. I started actively posting on the site and in particular wrote a post quite early on, on why the DNA analysis had to be wrong. The post was well received since it explained in layman's terms why the knife DNA was wrong (You should never increase the sensitivity of an analysis beyond the range of the instrument and method you used to make the sampling) and the bra strap was also wrong (You should never try to analyze a demonstrably contaminated sample). I not only read more and more but I then wrote to both Amanda and Raffaele. I was not surprised that Amanda did not reply but Raffaele did. I started to write to him. Fairly early on I asked Raffaele if there was anything I could do. It was then that I got contacted by a reporter from OGGI asking if I would do an interview. I hesitated out of respect for the Kerchers. Then John Kercher wrote an article in which he vehemently endorsed the conviction of Amanda and Raffaele making statements about the case which he simply should not have made. At that point I felt the other side needed to be heard and so I agreed to do the interview.

After the interview was published I received a series of wonderfully supportive e-mails from the group of people who were working to right this injustice. I also received a few e-mails from guilters some of which I still have not read. 'Zorba' wrote to the high ups in my university saying that I had no right to speak out and threatening vaguely what would be done if I was not dealt with. The university wrote back saying that as long as I was not claiming to speak on behalf of the university it was not their business – for which I am very grateful. Since then I have become part of the 'inner' circle and been made to feel very welcome. I was particularly pleased that the article was in Italian and therefore reached the most important audience, the Italians in general and the potential jurors in particular. I felt I did something to help turn the tide at that time.

Since then I have had a regular correspondence with Raffaele. It is a real old fashioned exchange of letters. I have been amazed how positive he has remained throughout this experience. Again I feel I have been able to help in a small way to make his life somewhat easier. In particular I have sent him copies of the most relevant posts from IIP and elsewhere which meant that he realized how many people were seriously involved in helping and support him and his family. I remember comments by Solzhenitsyn who said that knowing people were thinking about him made his imprisonment in Siberia less unbearable. At times I also sent posts to the main group to make sure that we all remembered that two of them have been wrongfully convicted and not just Amanda, who of course has been the media focus.

This text is supposed to answer why I got involved and why do I care so much. I have tried to analyze that myself. Part of it is a deep revulsion at the idea of anybody being put in prison for a crime they did not commit. Somewhere that came to me personally as being a 2nd generation Holocaust survivor. My parents were refugees from Europe in the late 1930's and all their parents (my grandparents) perished in the holocaust. I am a university Professor and always try to go out of my way to help students if I can. Here Raffaele gave me the opportunity to get involved and to write to him to help him get through this nightmare. That has made me feel good. There is also a tremendous feeling of camaraderie generated by the internet group. The enthusiasm, the commitment and most of all the warmth, makes this cause something one can feel really positive about especially since communally it does appeal that we are contributing to a positive outcome of the appeal. When I read the guilters complaining that the DNA report looks to have had contributions from FOA I take that as a tremendous compliment to the group and what it has been doing even though my contribution has been rather small.

Nigel Scott

I read the newspaper reports of the crime in 2007. When Amada and Raffaele were arrested I remember thinking that this was an unlikely scenario. When Rudy was arrested in Germany and brought back to Perugia, I wondered what sort of crime theory would put them all together.

British tabloid coverage was way over what would be allowed in the UK for a domestic case but I don't read tabloids so most of this passed me by. The first article that made a real impact was a Sunday Times Magazine piece on June 15th 2008. Edda and Kurt's interview in that article was credible and given the statistically remote possibility that a girl from Amanda's kind of background could ever be involved in this kind of crime, I believed it. I followed the trial and was convinced that Amanda and Raffaele were innocent. I was shocked by the guilty verdict and though I have never been personally involved in campaigning against judicial injustice, I decided that this was one case I couldn't ignore. The level of corruption, intimidation and media manipulation was simply breathtaking and I promised myself that I would stick with this until they were both freed.

I began posting on the Injustice in Perugia website and after a while, Joseph Bishop invited me to join the Facebook group, which I was honored to do. I have been shocked by the tactics of the Wikipedia muppets and the members of TJMK and PMF. I had not witnessed this

187

kind of mindless hate before. I like to think that I am a rational person so such displays of blinkered bigotry are hard to take. I have succeeded in getting several letters published in the UK media as well as an article about the case, which I wrote for a political magazine. I have also made countless comments on internet news pages.

I have tremendous admiration for Amanda and Raffaele's families and their persistence and dignity in their struggle as well as for the many supporters I have come to know through the Facebook group. And of course I feel for Amanda and Raffaele and the nightmare that they have been placed in by a deranged prosecutor and a corrupt system. They have shown immense restraint and have kept cool through a terrible ordeal. I have no doubt that they will go on to have successful and happy lives and will be able to put this behind them. I also believe that they will use the experience to help others in similar predicaments in the future.

I would like to see the corrupt officials and sloppy editors and journalists who exploited and benefited from this case sued, humbled, financially penalized and made to apologize for what they have done.

Aside from all of that, I would like to see some good come out of all this. I would like to see the Italian legal system reformed so that effective checks and balances exist to prevent cases like this from happening again. Last but not least, I would also like to pay a tribute to the innocent victim, Meredith Kercher and her family. As if their loss was not great enough, they were hoodwinked and conned by Italian prosecutors and lawyers who saw them only as a meal ticket without regard for the truth. May they find some peace at last and come to accept and understand what was done to innocent people in

Meredith's name. I cannot find words to express what I feel about the leaches who exploited the Kerchers.

I am a husband and father from North London. I have two grown up sons. I was born and schooled in Wales. I have been involved in politics at a local level for most of my life and I am currently a local councillor and school governor. I work for a health charity. My interests include music - mostly rock, jazz, blues, latin and country and football (soccer to those in the USA) and I support Tottenham Hotspur.

Paul R. Smyth

I got interested in the Knox-Sollecito case quite by chance. My wife and I were in Rome in May 2009 and so I was aware of the case and of the savagery with which the press treated Amanda and Raffaele. But I did not give the matter too much thought. I don't pay much attention to crime stories as a rule and, when I thought about it all, I thought Amanda and Raffaele were probably guilty. Why would I think otherwise? Italy seemed like a civilized country to me and the pair had good lawyers in what was superficially at least a fair and open proceeding. So when my wife later asked what I thought about the conviction, I said what I honestly thought: they were guilty. But Maureen suspected otherwise and uttered the fateful words: "You do research for a living; why don't you take some time over the Christmas holidays and look into the case more carefully."

And so I did. I expected to be able to report that Amanda and Raffaele were guilty in very short order. But things proved a good deal more complex than I imagined. I could tell within a few days that there were serious questions about the verdict and that the prosecution had not met its burden. But were Amanda and Raffaele actually innocent? That took a good deal more time to decide.

I read the National Academy of Sciences report on forensic evidence as a kind of useful background to my investigations and otherwise focused on the DNA evidence like a laser, reading materials from Bruce Budowle, the Crown Prosecution Service (UK) and the Forensic Institute in Glasgow. Soon after, I came across Mark Waterbury's material on Science Spheres. These readings convinced me that the DNA work done by Stefanoni was very wrong and entirely off the rails. Some people may have been surprised that Drs. Vecchiotti and Conti were so harsh in their assessment of Stefanoni's work. I honestly can say I was not surprised at all. The truth was there to see if you did your homework.

As I looked into other aspects of the case, I began to see a pattern developing: in every single instance, the defense was making the more plausible, research-based, convincing arguments. In January 2010, I found myself contemplating the utter absurdity of believing that there had been any kind of clean-up and decided that my views on the case were settled: the kids were completely innocent and had probably been framed. I immediately sent in the first of our contributions to the defense fund and began looking for other ways to contribute. I hooked up online with Jim Lovering, Candace Dempsey, and Joe Bishop and found my way on to Facebook and ultimately Injustice in Perugia. The rest, as they say, is history.

While I am quite confident in my views in cases where I have done my homework, I have to say that I was enormously gratified and pleased when I opened IIP one morning and found the first of Steve Moore's articles.

While Steve certainly added to my store of information, I had worked out his basic themes for myself. It was the fact that a 25-year veteran of the FBI agreed with my assessment of the case that was especially reassuring and wonderful.

I would also say that the years I spent teaching and the fact that my wife and I raised two sons to adulthood in East Lansing, a city we shared with 35,000 undergraduates, influenced my thinking. I always enjoyed teaching college students who, like Amanda, seemed to have big plans and an intense love of learning. "Neat kids," I called them—my highest term of honor. I also had a lively appreciation of what 20 year olds are like and knew that Amanda was a typical college student--just nicer and smarter than most.

'Bob'/ 'Sept79'/ 'Maryville'

I was aware in November, 2007 of the American student in Italy who was arrested for killing her roommate. I didn't give any real thought to the killing and arrest of the American other than the gnawing question of why would she have done this. After Amanda and Raffaele were sent to trial by Judge Micheli, I became interested in the case and started posting on Candace's blog in October, 2008. As I mentioned previously, my first reaction in 2007 and again in October, 2008 was WHY? Why would these young students be involved in a sexual assault/murder? Why would this couple of 6 or 7 days want to participate in a sex orgy with a drifter and Amanda's roommate? It made no sense whatsoever!

My first impulse is to seriously question an investigation when reading or hearing about some hideous crime where the accused is an unlikely person—

191

something way out of character. When scientific evidence is tenuous at best and there is no believable motive, bells and whistles go off! After quite a bit of posting/reading activity on Candace's blog and Perugia Shock, I was convinced of the innocence of Amanda and Raffaele before the start of the trial in January, 2009.

Heather Hales
I came to know Amanda and Raffaele's plight the day before the 2009 verdict…. A grad student commented that "if they find her guilty, all hell is going to break loose."…well it didn't…..I dove into whatever I could find on the internet and soon found injusticeinperugia. What I learned there motivated me to try to spread the word and recruit as many people as possible to the cause. I think that I felt somewhat of a connection to Amanda as I was oversees for a year when I was just 18. I was running around having fun, what happened to Amanda could easily have happened to me if I had been at the wrong place at the wrong time!

I found myself thinking about Amanda and Raffaele all of the time. I read articles and comments. I because infuriated at the "guilters!" I still to this day cannot understand what motivates people to behave in such a hateful way and to believe in a ridiculous fantasy just for the purpose of smearing two young innocent people!

I have lost most of my tolerance for the guilters and spend much less time on the comment boards arguing with them. There really is no point and they will crawl back in their holes when Amanda and Raffaele are released. The truth is finally coming out and I can't wait for them both to go home to their families. The ordeal has affected so many people close to the families and many who have never known them. I know that both Amanda and Raffaele are amazing people who will come out of this somehow better for it. They should never have gone through this at all! I hope with all my heart that the people who have been the guiltiest of abuse and dishonesty in this case will be brought to justice but I fear that will never be the case.

My heart and soul are with Amanda and Raffaele until they are home and also with all of the innocent family as well. I hope to meet you all in Seattle this fall!!!!

Cdyjuneau
I knew nothing about this case until about a year ago when I saw a brief interview with Amanda Knox's parents on the Oprah Winfrey show. I had a passing interest in a couple of controversial cases in Canada that ended up with the convicted people being exonerated so I was curious about this one. I supposed that the parents were just not able to accept the truth about their daughter.

I Googled and Googled and Googled. My Googling produced very confusing results. I kept finding old news reports that convinced me they must be guilty. The fact that Raffaele phoned the Carabinieri police after the Postal Police arrived and then lied about it could only imply guilt. The fact that Amanda showered in a bathroom without noticing blood that looked like it had been sprayed on the walls with a fire hose had to be conclusive. The fact that she had confessed to the murder. The fact that they had found her footprint in blood in the murder room. The fact that they had found Raffaele's running shoe footprint in blood. All these had to be conclusive of guilt.

Except that I had one advantage when deciding if they were guilty. By the time I was looking at these 'facts' a lot of time had passed. And each time I researched a bit further it turned out they were not facts. These 'facts' were false. And the trend was and still is that the prosecution's facts either did not stand up to scrutiny or were complete fabrications. And I began to question why the police were doing such a biased and unfair investigation. Guilty or not it was completely clear that Amanda and Raffaele were not being treated fairly. I was surprised; flabbergasted actually that so many people on the guilt side could not see this. I was certain that if this happened in Canada the prosecution and police would be crucified by the press and the public.

There were so many suspicious almost inconceivable things the police did. Like police experts wiping out hard drive alibi evidence faster than a hacker with attitude. Not collecting traffic camera videos from the area. The inspector saying he did not enter Meredith's bedroom when witnesses said he did and common sense would dictate entering to see if the person attached to the foot needed a doctor. Unless he already knew she was dead. And the police recording, bugging, and eaves dropping on everybody that could talk, grunt or fart but claiming they did not record the planned all night questioning of Raffaele and Amanda. And rushing out with a host of police to arrest Lumumba in the middle of the night based on Amanda's 'if I were a fly on the wall' statement. And Lumumba getting the same treatment. And Rudy having a history of armed burglaries and seriously threatening behavior that the police were aware of but did nothing about.

I am certain that Amanda and Raffaele never had even a hint of a fair investigation or trial. And I am equally certain that they are innocent.

Jason Leznek

It's a daily occurrence to read something bothersome in the news. Natural disasters, war, and other tragedies constantly remind us how helpless we can be, especially when something bad happens on the other side of the world. When something good happens, we all want to be a part of it and benefit from it. When something tragic happens, it is human nature to divert ourselves from it, to make sure it doesn't affect us personally. To not feel the pain others do. It's a rare and blessed opportunity when an average person can reach out and put themselves into a tragic situation and try with all their might and passion to help someone who is affected by a tragedy.

When I first learned about the tragedy I thought about Meredith, of course, and how painful it must be for her family and friends. To this day, I pray for Meredith and her family each morning when I wake up. I then thought about the case against Amanda Knox and Raffaele Sollecito; I hoped they were innocent, that it was a strange set of circumstances they were accused of being involved in, and that it was a shame it was happening. And then, as I watched Amanda's family tearfully expressing their feelings on the local television news, my thoughts turned to them…it became more than just an article on a web page. It became real. It became a family that could have been my neighbors. It could have been my family.

I've never involved myself in any business outside of my own. I've never reached out to a victim or a family affected by a crime or any other tragedy. As I learned more about the case against Amanda and Raffaele, however, I discovered very significant issues. I realized very early in my research they were not only innocent, but also very much targeted by a completely immoral prosecution and his team. The prosecutor himself was under indictment for similar misconduct in another case (he was found guilty) and should have never been involved in the case against Amanda and Raffaele. His lack of a moral compass or decency, his complete and utter disregard for truth and justice, his moral turpitude, his focus solely on making himself look good, and his total vendetta against Amanda, Raffaele, and their families was something I simply could not ignore.

Likewise, the behavior of his prosecution team and peers, including the head of the police investigation unit, his fellow prosecutors, and the forensics "specialists" showed either an utter contempt for truth, law, and process, or a total drowning in a sea of stupidity and incompetence. I fear they are the result of both.

With this knowledge, I needed to do something. I met a group of like-minded and passionate people through Facebook. We had the same goal yet with different backgrounds and skills. The bond we formed solely through the computer screen and keyboard is simply unprecedented. We each use the skills we have to drive the cause forward – to reach out to anyone who would listen and convince them of Amanda and Raf's innocence. I met Amanda's family, got to know them, and got to love them very quickly. I met Raf's sister online, and we quickly became close friends. Very clearly, this was no longer simply a news story on the television. These were my friends literally being held hostage by a corrupt megalomaniac with the power to get away with it. This was my family being forced to live through a tragedy for four years, shattering their dreams.

I have deep and complete sympathy for Meredith's family. I could never imagine what they have been going through – what they will continue to go through for the rest of their lives – in losing their angel. I also have sympathy for them that they have been sadly manipulated and misled by another power- and money-hungry prosecutor who has convinced them that they now have justice for Meredith, when in fact their tragedy simply continues and grows.

I know in my heart that this tragedy will be ending very soon. The truth will bring Amanda and Raf home, and bring closure to Meredith's family. I have confidence that the Italian legal system will not only correct a terrible mistake, but also do the right thing and condemn those power-hungry and malicious "defenders of justice" who have given a black eye to truth and justice everywhere.

I cry when the families cry. I will smile when Amanda and Raf are home. I will live when their lives go on as they always hoped they will.

Kaosium

I looked into it last summer to answer a question: why was Amanda being charged with calunnia for saying she was abused in police custody when the tapes were not available and it might cause her to serve six years in prison even if acquitted in her appeal? I was astonished at the debate that had developed about an issue I knew virtually nothing about. I found the wrong site first and read avidly, then decided to try another source and found the JREF thread. It looked to me like there was a decent case to be made for innocence, but the Massei Report was being translated and I assumed that information was necessary to make a decision, thus I put the issue away and decided to return to it in the fall, when the report would be available and the calunnia trial was scheduled to begin. It was quite possible to me the case made in court could have been imperfect but the accused still culpable, and I wasn't interested in whether they were just not guilty by law, but actually innocent. Guilty people must go free sometimes lest imperfect justice systems be corrupted and make the far worse error, but it doesn't have to involve me.

Returning to the issue in October it seemed something had transformed the debate, it had gotten especially ugly and I didn't understand why after reading the Massei Report: it was pretty clear the case had massive holes in it that had to be papered over with dubious conjecture I found appalling from a detached standpoint, however I'd learned a new case could be made in the appeal and it wasn't being made, despite the fact I knew those opposing her innocence had doubts about the trial as well from my reading in the summer. I thus tried to make a case for guilt and found IIP to read about the interrogation, and had an epiphany reading her note, it was like she spoke to me through the confusion, all that I'd read came to me in a rush and I thought I knew what happened, though I figured there might be something out there that I'd missed. So I created an account at JREF to ask the last questions I had, the things I'd seen happening at the other site baffled me, as they seemed fun and interesting enough months previous and had done a lot of work on the case, now they resembled hate cult. That didn't square at all with what I'd read earlier, nor did it make any sense, they were just college kids regardless that might have made a terrible mistake, not evil tyrants worthy of the merciless contempt I was seeing.

Soon my last questions were answered, and again I was mystified at how people could spend three years on this case and not realize the truth, it was convoluted and obfuscated by the man engineering the railroad and the reprehensible press coverage, but it was a puzzle that could be solved. I also was embarrassed I'd ever thought them guilty and ashamed I'd thought of them as simply mind candy to play with in my abortive 'guilt scenario.' I also realized they'd been smeared, Amanda especially, which had caused me to lose all interest in politics that once enthralled me when studying the Enlightenment in college, as it seemed that's all that media in democracy amounted to these days. These were two perfectly nice young people who'd been abused and made into monsters in part by what was once the tools of knowledge and the road to freedom. I rediscovered something of my youthful idealism and perhaps I can employ what I've learned since in a worthwhile struggle.

Rick Bonin
I first took note of the Meredith Kercher case in June of 2009. The tabloids were in full assault mode against Amanda and Raffaele, and I recall thinking, "They really don't look like the type to do this". But like many, I just assumed they were guilty, otherwise why would they be arrested and on trial? My early web searches turned up mainly Guilter sites like True Justice for Meredith Kercher and Perugia Murder File, and we all now know how persuasive these liars can be.

The case really captured my curiosity, and as I continued to search the web, I eventually found sites like Friends of Amanda and raffaelesollecito.org. Reading the endorsements by Amanda's and Raffaele's family, teachers and friends really turned my thinking around and I was virtually sure they had to be innocent. People that commit terrible crimes like this simply don't have this kind of loving family or friends like Madison Paxton. Just before the verdict in Dec. 2009, I discovered the Facebook groups. There I found others who felt like I did, but at the same time, I encountered the seedier side of the internet. In 2010 and into 2011, I devoured the books written by Candace Dempsey, Bruce Fisher, Mark Waterbury and Rocco Girlanda. These books, along with the Injustice in Perugia, Science Spheres and Perugia-Shock web sites, contained the facts I needed to strengthen my resolve. Even at work, I spent countless hours on Facebook, learning the facts of the case and defending the innocents against the Guilters, but also forming a bond with others like me who were standing up for Amanda and Raffaele and their families. Many, like me, had no connection whatsoever to these good people, but we all found ourselves fighting for them like they were our own family.

As I write this, most of the true Guilters have disappeared from the Facebook groups. A few of them even had enough character to stay around and admit they were wrong. I am really looking forward to celebrating the release of Amanda and Raffaele this fall with all my friends on Facebook. I think there will be a few virtual tears shed that day!

Michael Charles Becker

I was following it from a distance until the trial was half over and felt the odds favored Amanda and Raffaele being acquitted. I became involved with the case after the verdict, which left me shell shocked. I did not sleep the whole night of the verdict and spent the whole time on the internet trying to see if I had missed something and they could possibly be guilty. I quickly found all of the main players and found the whole tone on PMF and TJMK to be snide and repellent and FOA, Perugia Shock and Candace Dempsey's blog, plus the ridiculous case blog, and Science Spheres to be what shone out as the truth. I kept at the research for the next several days and was really wrung out and exhausted staying up every night, fitting in things during work.

I assembled my own timeline and main doc with links and quotes and info in a similar structure to what Bruce set up later in IIP mainly so I could keep my facts and sources straight when commenting online and I kept correcting it and adding to it day by day. I collected a lot of information from all the sites and a lot from comment section on Candace's blog - read ALL of them and had a history lesson in the War with the guilters and met all the names so to speak on both sides. Frank's blog had a similar dynamic but wilder. Somewhere along the line I coined the term "Guilters" and Bruce picked it up (and credited me, thanks Bruce!) and explained it on IIP.

Cathleen Krepps

My reasons for why their case touched my heart are, of course, personal: I had a beautiful blonde, blue eyed, funny, intelligent daughter (like Amanda) who travelled Europe and studied in London for a year. She never thought she was beautiful (she was) and did not see how many men sighed over her. She had a wonderful attitude toward the world - there were adventures to be had, and a stranger was a friend you had not yet met. She met people and ran into adventures and lived life fully. She died of an inoperable brain tumor.

As a parent I know the all-encompassing frustration and deep deep sadness of NOT BEING ABLE TO PROTECT your child. Amanda was caught up by her own belief in the goodness of people, and her belief that people would believe her. Her parents did not for-see evil in this awful case because they knew their daughter and her honest and earnest self, and besides, why would they suspect the police?

Of course these same reasons apply to Raffaele- He is a good kid, out for an adventure, and having fun. He met a beautiful girl and they had fun together. How could two ordinary good kids be caught in this nightmare? What puzzles me is that people don't realize that murderous sociopathic personalities do not arise out of a vacuum - there are signs all along during childhood. In Amanda's and Raffaele's case - there is NOTHING that would indicate crazy orgy murderous actions are in their future. They both have families and big groups of friends who believe them and love them. There are no neighbors who came out saying "I always thought she/he was a bit off, weird or creepy" NO! And those people love to come out and be interviewed. But not in this case.

The sad thing is that because these kids are caught in this web, most people think, then, that they must be guilty because they were caught in this web. Circular and crazy-lazy thinking.

I personally know what it is like to be caught in a government web: I submitted bills for services to the US government which were paid. I thought I was following all the rules, which were hard to understand. I reviewed and reviewed the rules, and was paid for several years. Then I asked for help just to be sure I was doing it correctly, and was turned in by a whistle-blower who wanted some of the action. Whistle-blowers get paid part of proceeds collected from these cases. Never mind that I had asked for help all along. I was threatened by millions of dollars in fines. We resolved it and I admitted no guilt. My lawyer is now a federal judge who still thinks I got the short stick in this case. So I do know the feelings that the world thinks I was a crook, that there was no way out, my reputation was shot, and that no one believed me.

When I read different comments by people about Amanda and Raffaele (actually mostly about Amanda-interesting that) on other sites I see many hateful words. People will see what they believe, not believe what they see. So, their belief that these two were guilty (never mind there was NO evidence in the room where the murder took place-- what did they do-- float??) will color everything they hear/see/read. They dismiss any contrary evidence because they simply cannot see it. It won't register.

I sincerely feel for Meredith's parents. This case became about Amanda and Raffaele, not poor Meredith. I am sure they feel push/pulled and want to think Meredith put up quite a fight and that it did not take only one crazed man to kill her. They will need to continue to believe that Amanda and Raffaele were involved.

I worry about Amanda and Raffaele for the time when they are released. I pray they can heal from the damage, and begin to trust the world again. It is hard to think that some in the world think you have committed a crime, even though you know you have not. I pray that these kids will be able to move forward. I hope they choose constructive actions and not let the scar of these years dictate their actions in a 'I will show them' kind of mentality. That is they will not decide to do bad things because the world thinks they are bad anyway. I worry about the pressures of books and movies and those greedy people who come out of the woodwork on these kinds of occasions. But then they come from good families and will have lots of support. They have my support and my belief that they are good people. I pray that is enough.

Susanna

In the late '70s I was enrolled at the "Stranieri" in the Etruscan Archaeology course they run every summer. Like Amanda, I am from the West Coast, had worked various jobs to save the money to do this, and was delighted to be in Perugia. It was one of the most important experiences of my life and I still consider myself very fortunate to have been able to achieve it. Much like Amanda, I think.

When I first read the headlines about AK and RS, I was intrigued because of my own Perugian experience. I--like most people--assumed that they must be guilty. Why? Because, like most people, I had no reason to doubt the Perugian authorities. Horrible story but, if one believed the news media, these were two drug-addicted (and probably sociopathic) kids. Terrible stuff happens (as in the Manson case) when drugs are involved.

When I went on line to look into the story, I found TJMK and PMF. And I was immediately struck; i) by the venomous and emotional attacks on AK and RS; ii) the irrational, evidence-free assertions of their guilt; and iii) the vicious attacks the "guilters" mounted against any poster who even hinted at the possibility of innocence or had the temerity to ask for evidence.

It was unclear why these complete strangers to AK and RS felt so strongly about them and were so convinced of their guilt. It seemed bizarre that utter strangers were so angry and worked up about a case in which they had no personal stake.

I tried to learn more about the huge PR campaign of the Knoxes that the "guilters" alleged, but was unable to find any trace of it on the internet. I visited Anne Bremner's site numerous times, looking for evidence of this juggernaut, but could find no information about it whatsoever. I began to suspect that there was no such campaign.

Then I watched an interview with Doug Preston, in which he described his experience with the prosecutor in the "Monster of Florence" case. I read his book and became very skeptical about Mignini's motivation in the Knox-Sollecito case.

I caught an interview on You Tube with Barbie Nadeau and was struck by her obvious assumption of guilt on the part of AK and RS; aren't journalists supposed to keep an open mind about the stories they cover? Yet it was completely obvious that Nadeau was actively pushing their guilt, through innuendo and a distortion of what I now knew to be the facts.

Then I discovered IIP and Perugia Shock and was able to study the facts of the case. I became persuaded by the factual evidence presented there (i.e. the lack of evidence) that Amanda and Raffaele could not have committed the crime. And I now am convinced that there was an outright conspiracy mounted against them by the Perugian authorities, led by Prosecutor Mignini.

I think that my change of attitude towards the case parallels that of most people who believe in the innocence of the two; people who take the time to look at the facts and stop paying attention to media lies and distortions ultimately have to conclude that AK and RS are innocent. So, that's my story, and I'm sticking to it! Thanks, and best wishes.

Andrew Lowery
First off, how I came to be doing this is related to what I was doing before; I'd spent my entire life as an artist of one type or another, mainly as an actor but sometimes as a composer, and I'd gotten a gig with a Shakespeare Festival that was going to Florence to perform. It was going to be one of those gigs where we all played a bunch of different parts (to cut costs) but I'd never been to Italy so what the heck? Anyway, we performed for several weeks and during that time I fell absolutely in love with Italy. It's difficult to explain what can happen to you there; let me just say that when you see the Duomo for the first time it does something to your head. When the time came to leave I looked at the rest of the Company and said "Home? Where's that?" With that I tore up my ticket and officially became an American Ex-Pat. I was pretty broke but I didn't care; I was sleeping on the banks of the Arno and sometimes in Hostiles but I didn't mind; my 'sense' was I'd left the prudery and puritanical sensibilities of conservative fanatacism behind. I felt free really for the first time and honestly I had no idea how dangerously naïve this kind of thinking could be, (rather I should say, "I was so intoxicated by the environment that I'd momentarily forgotten. Really, I'm old enough to

know better but trust me – it's an easy place to let your guard down.) Eventually I met someone who hired me to write copy for his company's website and also to work up a theme for an exhibition they wanted to create for their art gallery in Florence; in short order I moved into the gallery and the great adventure had begun. Over the next months we did an enormous amount of work together and I continued to absorb myself in the city of Florence - which is overwhelming. At any rate - after about 6 months something came up back in the states and I was forced to return home.

I read the first reports of a study-abroad student being murdered there and I was very, very sad. In my own naiveté, which I imagined mirrored that of the kids involved, I had come to believe the finer sensibilities of Italy, with all of its cultural sophistications, was a buffer against such crimes as these. Some of my favorite times there had been spent talking with Intl. students so I felt I knew these kids, what their dreams were and when I heard they had arrested an American student for the crime I just thought it was all such a waste, such a tragedy. Then a story floated up out of the investigation that this was a "sex orgy" or some kind of "ritual" with something "satanic" involved. I'd seen these kinds of accusations before right here in the States and most of them turned out to be fueled by an odd alchemy of hysteria, zealotry, ambition and professional incompetence. My sense was, "Nah. Some things definitely wrong with this." At the center of the gathering storm were two unlikely looking murderers, Amanda Knox and Raffaele Sollecito and when they started snagging and publishing harmless looking (to me anyway) pictures lifted from their websites and marketing those as some kind of evidence of psychopathic behavior it was pretty clear to me that this was an investigation that had gone out of control. I let things rest there thinking it was something that sounded like it was going to work itself out but it never did; the case was progressing, I started searching around the web when I came across the Friends of Amanda site which provided information and insight into the case as well as into Amanda herself that simply wasn't available anywhere else. Her story made me heartsick so I put together the first video, "Amanda Knox in her Own Words" and used pics of her set against her shaking voice as she tried to explain what was happening to her in front of the court. When I'd heard that after she made this heartrending and emotionally devastating statement the prosecutor belittled her and accused her of crying "Crocodile tears" I dedicated myself to helping her any way I could right there. Many others have heard this very moving statement and have had the same reaction.

So there was Candace Dempsey's wonderful blog where many, many remarkable and intelligent people constantly analyzed the case (she had been smart enough to close it down to keep the howlers in the 'guilter culture' out so some serious discussions could be held). Between articles and posts and monitoring the blog and working on her book it seemed she was going 24/7.

I found out later that yes, indeed she was; her contribution to all of this, including writing the first articles defending Amanda and Raffaele and bringing many, many new supporters into the fold, really can't be calculated. It's a privilege to call her a friend. At any rate I was concentrating on putting short films about the case together and posting them on the teatro33 YouTube channel and 'around' when I noticed a scientist was posting his grave misgivings about the prosecution's case on Frank Sfarzo's blog. At the time Frank's board wasn't monitored and he was viciously attacked; it was really something to see. Finally he gave credentials to try to keep doubters at bay but, as in most cases like this, 'facts' don't matter. He eventually gave up and started his own blog with an article called LCN DNA Profiling Part I, Canaries in the LCN DNA Mine. This was a profoundly disturbing analysis of the use of LCN DNA in the case and it covered many, many bases that had not been covered in the media at all. I started communicating with him via email and decided to have the articles translated into Italian and featured on a site "AmandaKnox.it". I wanted the site to look really, really special so, not being a web designer, I used a spectacular flash software design package available from Wix.com and worked for many hours to make the overall look as artistic as I could; the point was to appeal to Italian sensibilities. I believe Barbie Nadeau was so confused by this effort she once wrote something like "...supporters even put up a site that has nothing to do with the case...". We kept the site up in that form until the end of the first trial when she was convicted. That was a terrible moment.

During the first months after the conviction more and more people were finding out about the specifics of the case, starting their own support sites and blogs and otherwise getting onboard. Among these were highly credentialed professionals at the top of their fields, (like Dr Waterbury) and they all were upset enough about what was happening to these kids that they made time in their incredibly busy lives to help them out; they all have their own reasons but in the service of the greater good this case was about superstition vs. rational thinking; it had to be fought and it had to be won. One of these was an ex-FBI agent named Steve Moore. He'd written a series of articles for IIP and Bruce contacted me and asked me to put the site together featuring translations of Steve's blistering attack on the prosecution's case. If ever there was a glass ceiling that held the truth about Amanda and Raffaele's insane prosecution and conviction for murder in the peripheral vision of the general media it was Steve who shattered it to pieces and brought the case to center stage. So the site went back up featuring translations of Steve's articles along with Marks. Then there were hundreds of mail-outs of press releases to Italian media (which produced, as far as I know, nothing.)

There's much more but that's the beginning of it and then some I guess. Sorry; I just kind of got going but I must say I'm very proud to have been a part of it and to have helped in whatever small way I did; most of all though I'm proud of Amanda and Raffaele. I believe if it weren't for their light at the center of all of this tragic mess many of us would have given up hope; while I know the converse is obviously true it must also be said that it was they who lifted us and while they may never understand this I know it to be true. The rest - thank God - is now history.

Chris Halkides

I first become interested in this case when I read how much latitude the prosecution had basically to make things up in its closing remarks. However, what really got my attention was when nine DNA scientists wrote or signed a letter which took the prosecution's forensic case to task. It was very disturbing to me to see that crucial information was withheld from the defense. That is the opposite of good science. I stayed involved because I thought that my scientific training could help bring these issues to light.

Here are some of my take-home messages from this case. First, we should not believe the prosecution or the media when they broadly engage in character assassination. As in the Duke Lacrosse case, the defendants in no way, shape, or form resembled how the prosecution and some elements of the media portrayed them. Second, the existence of DNA evidence does not give the members of the jury license to check their brains at the courthouse door. DNA is still the best forensic evidence there is, but it has its limitations. Third, in the United States the appeals system is barely functional, and we have plenty of wrongfully convicted people in this country who would benefit from the kind of support that were rightfully shown to Amanda and to Raffaele. Fourth, if we allow the presumption of innocence and the standard of beyond a reasonable doubt as the bar for conviction to continue to erode, we will get exactly the criminal justice system that we deserve.

Jim Lovering
I followed the Meredith Kercher murder case from the start. After a few months, I could see that the police had staked their credibility to a false accusation and were scrambling to save face at the expense of two innocent people.

In March, 2008, I stumbled on Candace Dempsey's blog and read her interview with Doug Preston, who had an earlier run-in with Giuliano Mignini. Preston confirmed everything I was already thinking about the case.

I started posting on an Internet board that was dominated by people who believed everything the tabloids said about Amanda and hated her accordingly. I tried, in vain, to point out the many problems with the case. This got the attention of Chris Mellas. When he realized I lived in the area, he invited me to his home. I have since become friends with him and Edda and gotten to know Amanda's entire family. I went to Italy and met Amanda in prison.

When I got involved in the effort to help Amanda and Raffaele, I expected that they would be convicted in the first round of the legal process. But I also believed sustained public interest would eventually bring the force of reason to bear. I figured it would take at least five years, but I underestimated the power of the Internet and social networking. I did not realize how many intelligent, motivated people would devote their time to the quest for justice. I will always take satisfaction in knowing I was part of a team that helped correct a terrible mistake.

George

I must make a little premise to make better understand my personal moral position regarding the Perugia case. My native town is found not far from Perugia it-self, they share the same awareness about history and traditions, making them two provincial adversaries, with two hearts and one mind.

Having said that, I want to add that an event like the one occurred in Perugia to Amanda an Raffaele, made some rumor around the region, making my-self to sympathize immediately with them, I must confess that although I was born in Italy, I am somebody in full disagreement with some aspect of the Italian way of life, and it came natural to identify with their predicament, these sentiments, especially knowing the social and political stand which this case implied.

The Italian public is quite used to this kind of crime stories, and before they take position to support one side or the other, they want to make sure not to bid on the loser, here it is like a life game, some may win, some may lose and sometime the truth it is only a chance, but the unclear circumstances which brought this young couple involved deeper and deeper in being suspected of the hideous crime, built in my mind a sense of rebellion.

Because, the evidences seemed right away vitiated and fictitious, and the hype of the media on speaking about it in a prejudicial manner, made them even more trivial and inconsistent, but "dura lex set lex", which means "the law is hard but it is the law", as the antique Latin's used to say, and Amanda and Raffaele had to experience on their shoulders the hard meaning of such locution.

For one thing, the profile of Amanda and Raffaele was not that like the one as described by the prosecution, I saw double when I heard they being so infamously depicted as two monsters, but the picture was not there, I was perplexed about why he would not take account of the young age of the couple, from a parental and psychological point of view.

Actually the whole behavior of Amanda before the police gave me the first enlightenment of her innocence, but an occult power worked against her, and instead interpreting this irresponsible side of her personality as youthful and ingenuous, they went heavy on her, messing up not just the right order of the investigation, but also her precious existence.

Now the rest is history, thanks god they were able to affirm their absolute foreignness to the facts they had been imputed, and I sincerely hoped that one hundred percent, it did not make sense differently, now I am pondering about their judicial situation, was it better to get a sentence with a reasonable doubt in the first trial and just set free waiting for the appeal, or spend 4 years in jail to get a full acquittal? Big question, only Amanda and Raffaele know the answer.

It is well known that the Italian judiciary system works slow, because the character of Italians is litigious, which fill the courts with any sort of complains, but if you are patient and tenacious, eventually you are able to resolve your rights, but again, for some people may be an excruciating experience, and Amanda and Raffaele proved it to extreme.

Colin Connaughton, London
Like most people, I read about the murder of Meredith Kercher in the media shortly after it happened. I saw the media reports soon after about Amanda and Raffaele sharing a kiss outside the house which the police had cordoned off as a crime scene. I was shocked by the animosity displayed in the reporting against Amanda and Raffaele. The couple struck me as being two ordinary and nice looking young students who were disoriented and stunned by the terrible events which had occurred. Like ordinary good people they were making the best of it and it was obvious that Raffaele was trying to comfort Amanda who was clearly upset.

When I learned that Amanda and Raffaele were arrested for the murder I was so skeptical that I nearly laughed. There was no way that those two nice students were involved, I thought. And what on earth could be the motive? It didn't make sense. I'm old enough and experienced enough to know that police are sometimes like a lot of people in this world. They like to take the easy option and they are sometimes inclined to suspect people just because they happen to be close by. I've seen examples of this in my own life. I decided to wait for the evidence which I knew in advance would be flawed or non-existent. In the meanwhile I was dismayed to read silly tabloid reports about 'Foxy Knoxy' and her so-called 'antics'. To me, the so-called 'antics' were perfectly normal behavior of innocent but individual people. Guilty people would try to blend in, keep a low profile, and do whatever they could not to attract attention. I was shocked again when the judge made public statements, long before the trial started, about what (in his view) had happened and that Amanda and Raffaele were guilty. How could he possibly know what had happened and how could he be allowed to talk like that before the trial had even started? So I decided to do some research and perhaps help the side of innocence in what was clearly a trial by media.

kindlekitten
I became interested and got involved with this case for a variety of reasons. First and foremost was the simple incredulity that a young from a seemingly normal background would become involved in such a lifestyle was very difficult to believe. What really pushed my buttons were several; I was a young female soldier

stationed in a foreign country (18 in Germany) and watched a friend of mine get into trouble with the German Polizei over what was basically cultural misunderstandings. The trouble that she got into was nothing remotely similar to what these kids have gone through, but I can see how it could have gotten very out of line very quickly. Additionally, I have hosted quite a few foreign exchange students and have seen firsthand how cultural issues can become blown out of the water very easily. What has kept me involved has been the remarks made by many that it is "obvious" that she has been guilty all along solely based on stories and remarks made by journalists and persons perceived to be in charge have made. If anyone has ever been falsely accused of doing or saying something that they did not (which I have been), having others stand up for you is invaluable. I think that there are some personalities that for whatever reason attract a certain amount of scrutiny that the norm does not generate. I'm not sure if this is a particular zest for life, a way they carry themselves, or what exactly the issue is, but it happens. I've been told more than once that I probably would have been burned as a witch if I had lived in a different time, simply because I tend to march to the beat of a different drummer. I think it very likely that Amanda embodies this as well.

LondonJohn
Funnily enough, I first became involved in the internet discussion of this case as a loose believer in the guilt of Amanda Knox and Raffaele Sollecito. I'd read a book (Darkness Descending) which seemed at the time to make a strong case for guilt (although I subsequently discovered that there were a number of crucial

inaccuracies in the book), and I thought I would scan the net to seek answers to a few questions that were in my mind. I soon discovered three things: firstly, the facts of the case were not as I had believed; secondly, the available facts did not support an argument for guilt; and thirdly, there was an intensely polarized debate taking place on the internet about the case.

The more I read - and participated in - the online debate, the more I realized that people on one side of the debate were broadly interested in open discourse, objective analysis, and critical thinking. In contrast, most on the other side of the debate were closed-minded, dogmatic, fiercely defensive and logically unsound. The former group represented the pro-acquittal (or pro-innocence) standpoint; the latter group were the pro-guilt faction. The more I learned and participated, the more certain I became that Knox and Sollecito should never be convicted of Meredith Kercher's murder, and that in fact they were most likely completely innocent. And I suppose I feel a small twinge of pride at having been a proponent of acquittal (and, increasingly, of innocence), but I defer totally to Bruce and his group for their unrelenting determination and devotion to articulating and advocating a just and rightful cause. Thank you for your huge efforts.

Gilbert (AKA European Neighbour)

A few remarks about myself: I am an architect in Vienna, Austria, half a century fulfilled. We have four children, three girls and one boy. Our eldest daughters (twins) are now a few months older than Amanda in November 2007 (for me still very young, although officially "adult"). I missed the first two years (barely remembering short news about VERY strange accusations four years ago by sources from a) police, b) tabloids c) Italy, therefore enough reasons to think like ????????). I got informed a few days before the verdict and consequently I was immediately shocked by the insane decision. I began to write letters to Capanne and Terni. It has resulted in me becoming a regularly pen pal with Raffaele, because he wants to exercise German language. I joined IIP early, nickname european neighbour.

Being European: Europe is a work in progress from a union to a federation or something similar new, therefore I felt responsible for an insane incident in a neighboring "federal state" and a European disgrace. I had to learn that we made progress in economic issues, but regarding justice systems there is still confusion and especially Ital has many flaws, also confirmed by rankings of the ECHR, which includes all European states also outside of the EU! But there is unfortunately a disadvantage of being American too: The assumed change of the American as the victim of the assault and the English girl as the victim of the judiciary would obtain a different result: To defenders of the Italian system (unjustified) arguments like death penalty, high incarceration rates, Guantanamo etc could not be provided.

Doing the first time: Regarding AKRS I did some things the very first time in my life: I did neither write letters to unknown persons in prisons before, nor I wrote letters to newspapers or to the mayor of Perugia who even responded etc, nor I joined Facebook and last but not least I didn't join an internet forum before.

About IIP: Initially I didn't appreciate an additional blog because I would have preferred to improve or to enlarge an existing blog I already noticed: From Mark's science spheres to Sforza's Perugia shock and especially Jim Lovering's FOA. I was primarily interested in information about the further proceedings, not so in "evidence", because discussing it is to me nearly insulting intelligence. But after I got rather soon a pen pal of Raffaele I realized that even he or Bongiorno would not be able to predict further developments because of the unpredictability of the Italian system. After the rearrangement of the IIP site in May 2010 I joined rather early to the forum. I never cared about the background of this site or of Bruce Fisher himself, if he is real or if it's organized by Marriott or Simon etc, never mind, the more the better. Occasionally I could provide contributions and I have always appreciated to be in good company, because most of the members are decent and honest.

Black and white: In most issues I prefer the color gray, being ambiguous, looking at something from different sides etc. But in this case the two sides are exceptionally clear: There isn't even a little fire which causes smoke because there is only fog. It's simple instead of complicated, either good or bad, intelligent / stupid, honest / dishonest, true / false, sophisticated / primitive, enlightened / superstitious, open minded / provincial, emancipated / misogynist, scientific / illusionary, polyglot / monolingual etc. And I am still wondering why people can even consider and why media can still rely on the latter parts.

Lisa Rieger

I'm still scratching my head over the way I got wrapped up in this case, which was Facebook. The same type of social networking that was detrimental to Amanda and Raffaele in the press.

I got involved late. When I heard the guilty verdict of the first trial, I didn't even know Amanda was still in jail. I thought her case had been resolved over a year before without trial, but I recalled immediately the tender kissing scenes that had been played continuously on TV back then. I felt confused – I wondered what the evidence was so I started researching. Even after almost a yearlong trial I was amazed how hard it was to locate accurate facts about the crime and shocked to see how the evidence presented by the prosecution evolved over time. Most articles were drenched with sensationalism.

I would have to say that what spurred me on further was the extremely shoddy journalism, not only in the tabloids but also by supposedly educated people at formerly quality sites such as The Daily Beast and Newsweek. In those sites I saw good, hard-working family and friends of Amanda and Raffaele vilified. I saw people like Douglas Preston, Frank Sfarzo, and Steve Moore ridiculed for their hard work not only in the press but also on hate sites run by mostly anonymous posters. I'm just scratching the surface of the totality of the hateful posting I read based on falsehoods perpetuated by a frenzied mob of "journalists.

I did lots of posting of information I found about the case to the Free Amanda Knox site on Facebook where later I saw Bruce Fisher posting. A few months after that he asked for all those links to my sources. Later he created the excellent site "Injustice in Perugia", an incredible source of information.

I emailed Dr. Mark Waterbury with some questions I had about the case and he replied. Through emails we got to know each other a bit and I then did research on articles in Italian and British tabloids written immediately after the murder along with the work of some other journalists over time, and sent my findings to him. He wrote the book "Monster of Perugia: The Framing of Amanda Knox." Dr. Waterbury graciously listed me in his acknowledgments page for some of the interesting facts I found. I was thrilled.

I want to thank Amanda and Raffaele and their families. I learned so much because of what happened in Perugia. Also for their strength of character through almost four long years, showing us all that perseverance pays off, and making it so clear to me personally that time really does march on even through terribly dark times. I wish nothing but the best for them both for the rest of their lives.

Randy N

I became interested in this case because of the strange circumstances being written about it although I did not follow it closely in the beginning. Later on I decided to look for more information on the case and I did that with the notion that the defendants were probably guilty as I was unaccustomed to believing that the police and courts simply got things that wrong. I searched the web and forums and watched the news magazine stories and I began to get a strange feeling that something was very odd here which caused me to look even more closely. I soon became aware that there were sites actually for and against guilt on the internet and did some study at each. I tended to favor for guilt except that the arguments being made for guilt often failed the "smell test" for me and they left me with more questions than answers. I soon was leaning towards what facts were showing me and that in fact the truth seemed to be almost certain that Amanda and Raff were innocent.

When the Massei report was finally translated I no longer had any doubts that the defendants were absolutely innocent. This document alone is stunning and must certainly become an example for law schools as a how not to. As a finding of fact it is outrageous for the judge to ask us to "imagine" and use terms like "in theory" and it is likely...I was astonished at the lack of real evidence in the case. That is when I became involved in earnest and wrote letters to everyone I could think of who could help shine a light on the grave injustice taking place in Perugia, Italy. By now it was clear to me that the prosecutor was using this case to deflect attention away from his own trial for abuse of office. And when I realized how the Italian justice system worked wherein the prosecutor leads the investigation then things quickly came together as to how such an unlikely crime with no real facts had ever been allowed to happen.

During the appeal I was convinced that the innocents would be freed. This time it was because of the prosecutions verbal attacks that told me even they understood they had been revealed as having no case. They offered no TOD, no weapon, no witnesses, and this time it was finally confirmed that the DNA evidence was not only unreliable but may possibly be completely contrived against these defendants. Finally they offered as a motive and even pleaded for the court to increase the punishment because of NOTHING! There was no motive. This was the final outrage and another example of depth of perversion they would allow into this case. All for the protection of ego.

We knew these DNA facts long before the independent expert report, but that report removed any doubt as to the depth of action that was taken against these two defendants and even the experts claimed that the erroneous DNA results may have come from contamination but that they could not rule out corrupt action as another possibility. After in depth study of this case there is no doubt in my mind that the police and prosecutor made a rush to judgment and when facts later revealed their mistakes that they simply decided to ignore the facts and make up their own "truth" about the case. They have failed completely in justice for Meredith Kercher and they failed completely by jailing AK and RS for almost 4 years for a crime they never committed and finally they failed all the families involved by prosecuting a case that showed the world that there are still modern day witch trials in Perugia, Italy at least.

Thanks for your hard work in providing several comprehensive web sites that allowed so many articles and analysis by several experts and that they could come together and be freely studied by all. This case shows what can happen when absolute power is allowed to go unchecked. I hope for Italy's sake that they look closely at how this ridiculous case was allowed to happen and that they use it to investigate the corruption that it so shockingly reveals.

Lisa in the UK
The news about Meredith's death was extensively reported in the UK, as was Amanda and Raffaele's arrest. I kept wondering what it was all about. The story as reported made no sense at all. I could not see why two highly intelligent, good looking young kids from good

homes with everything to live for would team up with a deadbeat drifter who they barely knew on the spur of the moment to kill their friend Meredith in a bizarre, satanic sex game; it was absurd. I hunted for the facts and found that there was extensive evidence tying Guede to the crime and nothing at all to implicate Amanda and Raffaele other than the highly suspect knife and bra clasp. After the guilty verdict in '09 I felt devastated. I had stayed up that night with my Mom hoping for a NOT GUILTY verdict. I could not sleep all night thinking of how Amanda and Raffaele must feel, not to mention the anguish of their families. I began writing a letter to Amanda immediately and sent it off to her in prison. I rang radio stations to speak out about what I saw as a huge injustice. I wrote to Senator Clinton to urge her to give Amanda's family support and my Mom and I made numerous calls to the Italian Embassy in London to voice our concerns about this unsafe verdict. Via Facebook, I got in touch with fellow supporters and Friends of Amanda. I continued to write to Amanda regularly throughout.

Peter Popham interviewed me for the *In dependant* newspaper in October 2010; that is where the photo of me in the FREE AMANDA T-shirt comes from. Hopefully my quote, "Common sense tells me that if there are four people in a room and there is a big struggle and one person gets stabbed in the neck, there's going to be an enormous amount of blood and an enormous transfer of DNA, and it shouldn't be very difficult to tie those people to the scene. And the fact that there is absolutely nothing to tie Amanda and Raffaele to that room at the time of the murder seemed to me to indicate that they are innocent." got through to people.

They always say that we are not individuals but are intrinsically linked and yet in this rat race of a world, one always feels very separate and alone. However working for this cause has given me a tangible sense of our interconnectedness. When Amanda and Raffaele were found guilty: I felt it as if I was there, as if I was them. As they waited for the Appeal Court verdict, I once again felt their tension, their dread and their hope as if we were one. And now I share their excitement for the future and joy at being free as if I am again part of them. This ordeal had shown so many of us, that we are not alone and together we can achieve so much.

It is quite obvious to me that the Knox's are an amazing family and Amanda an inspirational person. Her heartfelt thanks to all of us who saw through the lies and who sought the truth and spoke up for her was incredible... It was a pleasure to be on board and I will never forget the folks I met during this campaign.

God works in mysterious ways indeed!

Werner Gompertz
When the news was reporting the murder in Perugia in Nov. 2007 I did not pay any attention. Another murder, and the police will deal with it, I thought. It was not until summer 2010 that I started to pay attention, when a friend of mine expressed his outrage about the innocent girl falsely accused and convicted. His outrage was heightened by the thought that the American State Department did nothing to help. That made me start reading about the case, and, while at first I found a babble of voices with different claims all over the Net, the one constant was that the comments on blogs were for the most part intensely hateful. Anyone expressing the

possibility that she may be innocent was reviled. I had never felt such intense hatred for anyone, no matter how despicable their deed. I also discovered that the hatred was not based on any sound reasons. There were quite a few references to those "demon eyes" that told you she had to be a murderer. Then there was the oft expressed opinion that, even if she is not guilty, she has to be imprisoned to make up for Guantanamo or American treatment of third world people in general. There were mentions of Cavalese and of the arrogance displayed by American tourists who visited Europe. That is when I decided to investigate for myself and once I discovered the Injustice in Perugia website, I knew my confusions would be resolved. Steve Moore's articles were very compelling, and then I continued to learn more details, such as the facts about the insane prosecutor who accused all sorts of people of being devil worshipers and jailed those who disagreed with his theories. Then I read Monster of Florence and I realized that Mignini was even crazier than I thought. Doug Preston's book was only tangentially related to the Kercher murder, and only at the end. Preston did not write with a view to influence anyone's mind in the Kercher murder case, though he helped me to understand the conditions in that region which led to the culture of corruption that produced the injustice. Guilters often ask how it could be that the Perugian authorities would go to so much trouble to frame an innocent American student. I often refer them to Monster of Perugia and a few have actually taken my advice and read it, and it may have changed a few minds.

I must add that my convictions were strengthened by arguing on various blogs with some very determined guilters. When I was first challenged with the statements that supposedly proved Amanda was lying, I admit I did not have the answers. Even the bald assertion, "Innocent people don't lie" challenged me and I had to dig deeper. So I learned about false confessions, and about the Reid technique. I must admit that my strong traditional views about punishment have been tempered by a realization of how easy it is for the police to get a confession based on their interrogation techniques. If I needed any more convincing after reading Mark Waterbury's book, it came from reading that guilter bible, the Massei report. I actually felt bad for Massei and thought what a pitiful excuse for a judge he must be. His reasoning was no more logical than that of the commenters on blogs who used the drugs-and-sex-games theories to construct the most absurd and fanciful scenarios.

With the court decision freeing the captives, we all rejoiced. Yet the struggle continues, with Ann Coulter and Nancy Grace still spreading falsehoods that are passed on to their adoring but clueless fans. As Candace Dempsey said, "Some people won't take 'innocent' for an answer."

That, briefly, is my journey from indifference to understanding. I never for a moment considered the possibility that Amanda and Raffaele are anything but innocent once I focused my attention on the case about fifteen months ago.

wald1900
I recently joined the Facebook cause in support of Amanda Knox and Raffaele Sollecito, two students studying in Perugia, Italy who were convicted last year (unjustly, I believe) of murdering Knox's roommate, Meredith Kercher. Shortly after I posted the link to my

profile, a friend pinged me back with the following message: "You're still on about that?"

Several months ago I had shared my interest in the case with this friend, mentioning that I thought the two had gotten a raw deal and expressing hope that their conviction might be overturned on appeal.

That this friend would now be surprised (and, from her tone, incredulous) that I still followed the Meredith Kercher story took me aback. Oddly, I felt defensive; as though my interest was somehow suspicious and I had been caught red handed engaging in a shameful self-indulgence. In the finest tradition of thin-skinned petulance, my mind began cycling through the list of arguments that justified my fascination and proved - proved, I say - that every right-thinking person should be as interested in the Kercher murder as I am.

It was as I completed about the twentieth lap in the course of concentric circles I was walking in my office that I realized that I had actually been muttering under my breath and gesticulating at invisible debate opponents who'd taken up seats in the bleachers of my mind.

For whatever reason, the Meredith Kercher story has gotten under my skin. An inclination to midnight monologues directed at my dog (who, by the way, now agrees with me) and my cavalier use of the term "right-thinking person" are symptoms of just how deeply this story has wormed its way into my mind. Intellectual honesty compels me to concede that they might not be healthy symptoms. Moral honest compels me to admit that I'm hooked.

My interest is, admittedly, odd. I do not know Amanda Knox or Raffaele Sollecito personally, nor am I acquainted with anyone who does. While they are convicted of horrible crimes, Meredith Kercher's murder is not outside of the normal "bandwidth of horror" presented to each of us every day on the evening news. Third world infant mortality, sex trafficking from the East Block, the plight of baby seals or bigotry in my own home town all, arguably, produce victims more worthy of my time and interest. Yet every day I find myself doing a Google search on "Amanda Knox" to catch up on the latest developments.

What I learned about the evidence supporting the couple's arrest and conviction appalled me. In fact, my Kercher-meter now reads a bright red "Mad as hell"

So, why do I care? For me, the story has become about more than Amanda Knox, Raffaele Sollecito or even, Meredith Kercher. For me, the story is about how human beings can be wicked.

It is about how human beings can auger themselves into untenable positions, and become so invested in their own dogma that the option of sending two innocent young people to prison for a quarter of a century is preferable to admitting that they were wrong.

Margaret G Ralph

On a usual November morning in 2007 my cell phone was bouncing around on the kitchen table; that infamous day Amanda Knox was being questioned by Italian Police Authorities in Perugia, Italy.

Three consecutive text messages were from my daughter, Meghan asking me: "Did I see the news on TV?" "Did you see Amanda Knox" "Mom, she's being accused of murder!"

Since the beginning of November 2007, the time of Amanda Knox's arrest, I have been a devoted supporter for Amanda and Raffaeles' Innocence. I never doubted her innocence or faltered from this belief.

The days following the horrific news I literally spent hours watching my home videos taken during the 2 years Meghan and Amanda played soccer together for Seattle Prep.

I did not see a player who "needed to be the center of attention" nor did I see a player who "stood on the sidelines displaying odd behavior". In fact in the fall of 2005, Amanda Knox was recognized by Division AA as 'Top defender' from Seattle Prep High School and quoted in the Seattle Post Intelligencer Newspaper as a "dedicated and solid team player."

I remained anonymous in my unwavering support for Amanda and Raffaele so that I could also honor the privacy of my children. My son Brendan was attending Seattle Prep at the time and he participated in writing letters to Amanda during those first 2 years before her trial. Whenever possible, I donated whatever I could whenever I could and I continue to post my beliefs of their innocence and the overturn of their appeal, on many U.S. and UK blogs.

IN SUMMARY:

"My thoughts were, given Judge Mignini was in in a position to decide the ultimate fate of Amanda's and Raffaeles lives, then Judge Mignini owed it to Amanda

and Raffaele to "look into their eyes" and hear and listen to Amanda and Raffaele speak the truth in their own words ...

Judge Mignini could not bear to do this one act and by NOT doing so, this told me that Amanda and Raffaele did not deserve to have their fate of their lives decided by such a despicable coward."

I am no longer anonymous and haven't been for over the last 2 years and will forever stand up and defend their innocence. I deeply came to love and respect both families and look towards Edda as an amazing mom and Curt and Chris as amazing dad and step-dad; most profoundly has been the impact that Amanda has had on me personally; the courage, integrity, and the spirit within her soul that defines what it truly means to be an amazingly solid human being.

All your supporters I have been privileged to meet (either in person or through cyberspace), love you unconditionally and this love has bonded us together for life!

Through all the emotions we (your supporters (share together we also NEVER LOST SIGHT OF MEREDITH KERCHER and we acknowledge and pray for Meredith and her family always.

Thank you Amanda and Raffaele (and families) for teaching me that Truth is not only Love but Freedom.

Mark C. Waterbury, Ph.D.

Over the years of Amanda Knox's wrongful and unlawful incarceration I was impressed by her gentle responses to the often hateful acts directed at her, and by what appeared to me to be her efforts to remain herself, despite immense pressure to conform to various and sundry dark expectations. To me, her famous, "All you need is love" shirt made perfect sense. She seemed almost grimly determined to respond to hate with love, believing that her love would carry the day in the end. I hoped that she was right, but felt that she could use a little help along the way.

I followed the newspaper coverage about the events in Perugia, Italy from when the news first broke of a murder under unusual circumstances. I recall reading that a young woman, a local college student, was the roommate of a murder victim. When that woman was arrested for the crime, my concern grew because it didn't seem probable. When Rudy Guede was subsequently arrested for the same crime, I was relieved that finally matters had been righted, but of course, it did not happen, and the Perugian authorities performed their famous swap out. The path things were on did not make sense in some fundamental way.

Wanting to learn more and frustrated by the superficial mainstream press coverage, which typically devoted three quarters of each article to reciting the prosecution's charges, leaving very little room for real content, I looked for better news sources online and found the difficult-to-follow but cleverly written Perugia-Shock blog of Frank Sfarzo. After several months I made some anonymous comments in that blog, providing brief analysis of some of the forensic evidence from a scientist's perspective. Immediately, they were attacked, not merely criticized, on every imaginable basis. The attacks appeared to be an attempt to bully me, along with everyone else who questioned the evidence, into silence. From that point, of course, I had to learn and write still more.

Reviewing technology has been one of my jobs and passions over the years, and much of what I saw set off my pre-wired alarms: Exaggerated claims, misrepresented results, I saw the trappings of science without the substance. The forensics results were being manipulated, and so, too, it appeared was the rest of the case. This thing on the other side of the world, in another culture and language, was just plain wrong.

I had no standing in the matter and no platform from which to speak, but I began to think about how I might play the role of the butterfly of the butterfly effect flapping my wings to tamp down a hurricane, in this case.

Towards the end of 2008 I set up first blog on the case, a simple, free website at www.freeaman.001webs. It gave me a place to post information that I thought would be useful without wasting time responding to scurrilous fire. It became a kind of a chess game for me, trying to use my words to deflect events. By the summer of 2009 I had set up www.sciencespheres.com and written a series of articles about the DNA evidence under the heading "Canaries in the DNA Mine Shaft." Those articles were distributed to thousands of people by an early Facebook group and on other blogs, including one in Italian.

Soon after those articles I first met Chris and Edda Mellas, and their frankness and demeanor further convinced me that Amanda was no wild child, but a good, kind young person caught up in a whirlwind of self-serving officials and sleaze merchants.

I learned that the Italian people respond better to things that are written with some flair, rather than to recitations of fact. Also, there were already website resources that carefully went through the evidence, so I decided to lean toward a dramatic, and some would say melodramatic style while at the same time trying to add value from my scientific background. The material seemed to lend itself to using outrageous analogies, because that seemed the best way to capture the shear outrageousness of what was taking place. After writing a dozen or so articles, and still not feeling like I had shown the whole picture or done all that I should do, I began work on The Monster of Perugia – The Framing of Amanda Knox, working on it full time. I had never intended to write a book on the subject, it was almost as if it had written itself in my subconscious. At times that process was tremendously difficult, but the effort brought me back to my writing, and for that I will always be grateful.

Diane Lutz

I was much like Amanda when came to study in Italy in 1979 as part of a summer abroad program. I returned to Italy in 1986 and I have been living here ever since. I now have a teenage daughter. Why did I get involved in this case? I got involved for a few different reasons. I could have been Amanda. My daughter could have been Amanda.

I love Italy and the Italians and this case continues to break my heart. Although I only found out about the case in the summer of 2010 I couldn't believe the character assassination and deception that was unfolding in the media. I was incensed especially by the reports of the expat American journalists who said so many things about the trial, about Amanda and Raffaele and about Italy that I knew were inaccurate and misleading. I felt I needed to do something since I was living in Italy. I attended 5 hearings. I hope the encouragement I gave to Madison by the way of a smile and a hug helped in some small way.

Sarah Snyder
My involvement in Injustice in Perugia taught me tremendous lessons both about the power of a group and an individual. Before we organized into a grassroots group of supporters there was little hope we would have made much impact alone. By becoming an organization it lead down roads of greater direction, action and an actual goal of seeing the wrongful convictions overturned. Fighting against the early perceptions from an international media witch hunt and the lies of a corrupt prosecution, police and forensic team was a herculean task. Concerted efforts were made to counter all the lies and misinformation that had been spread online and in papers. We became the foot soldiers in changing and educating public opinion on this case. Letters were sent, contacts made, press releases distributed and articles written on topics not covered in the press. The group dynamic made this possible. Through the group there was camaraderie, numbers and we were not in the struggle alone. There were brainstorming sessions to bounce ideas

off of each other, encouragement to give things a try and ideas on what we could do to help. Injustice in Perugia played a large role in informing people of what a ridiculous and corrupt case of injustice this was and our efforts helped create a tide of change in people understanding what went down in Perugia.

Injustice in Perugia also showed me the power of an individual voice. We all can do more than we may realize. Many of us stepped out of our comfort zones and took chances in our efforts to help in ways we had no prior experience. Many jumped in knowing that someone had to do something and it can't be left always to other shoulders. Everyone helped in the best way they could, with their own individual talents and skills. I met some of the finest, most intelligent and kindest people I have in my life in this group. It was an honor to work with them in helping to correct this injustice.

Doug M

I first heard about the Murder of Meredith Kercher shortly after it occurred, although I did not pay too much attention at the time. I read a few newspaper reports, which said that a young woman was killed as part of a violent, drug fueled sex game. My initial reaction to this was disgust and a bit of sadness. I thought: "What are kids getting involved with these days?", and did not really take much interest beyond that.

As time went by, I was vaguely aware there was a trial, and assumed the three people charged were guilty. In my mind, it was still a story about these students who were into strange acts, including violent sex where people were threatened with knives, and hard drugs. Not very pleasant to read about. However, at around the time of the 2009 verdict in the first trial, I started seeing some stories and online comments where people were saying that Amanda and Raffaele were not guilty of the crime. I did not understand that, they were there for the sex game, right? How could they be innocent? So I started reading up on the case, mostly to try to understand how there could possibly be a question, especially when the murder was committed in the home that was shared by the victim and one of the defendants.

The more I read about the case, the more confused I became. The facts were much more unclear than I had expected, especially when I learned that Amanda and Raffaele were claiming they were not even present at the crime scene. What!? That shouldn't be hard to prove. Rudy Guede's story of being on the toilet when another man came in and killed Meredith was obviously not true, but what actually happened? I got more interested – it was becoming a mystery. I started reading everything I could find on the case, but could not understand how the guilty verdict was arrived at. "I must be missing something", I thought, because a court found them guilty. I kept seeing people online saying "read the 400+ page Massei motivation report, that will tell you about all the evidence that Amanda Knox and Raffaele Sollecito are guilty". There was so much vitriol toward Amanda and Raffaele, but particularly Amanda. So I downloaded and printed the whole Massei report, and read it over 3-4 days. Much to my surprise, on each point of evidence, the judge would accept the prosecution version of what it meant, and dismiss the alternative explanation given by the defense. The farther I got into the report, the more confused I got – where was this convincing evidence that these two people were even there, much less killed anyone? When I finished the report, I had to go for a walk and think, because I was astonished at what I had read. I didn't know for sure what happened, but I was sure that report did not explain any clear case that Amanda or Raffaele was involved in any way.

Now I had to understand what was going on. I read two books on the case, and read all I could find about the case online, including the arguments from those convinced of guilt, and innocence. Although I was sure the court did not have proof of guilt beyond a reasonable doubt, people kept talking about Amanda's "confession", and how she accused an innocent man. So I read Amanda's statements, and was shocked at how they had been interpreted. These were obviously not confessions or accusations – she was clearly confused. I read transcripts of Amanda's interviews and watched tapes of her testimony, and became more and more alarmed. I realized that Amanda and Raffaele were not only innocent, but at every step the facts had been completely twisted – this was not just a misunderstanding, they had been manipulated and railroaded.

Now that it had become clear to me what had happened, I felt compelled to do something about it. It was disgusting to see people campaigning to keep Amanda and Raffaele in jail, when they hadn't done anything wrong. Well, if those people could post online, telling lies about these two kids, I could help by countering those posts – the truth would be my weapon. When I first came across the "Injustice in Perugia" website, I thought the name was kind of strong, since no one could be sure what had happened in this case, right?

But the more I learned, the more I realized there *was* a true injustice, and we **had** to change it. I am not an attorney or DNA expert or scientist, but by using the internet, I could educate people on the case, and hope that, in some small way, I could help to change things.

Along the way, I found there was a wonderful group of people that had come to the same conclusion that I had, and were also trying to set the record straight about what happened to Amanda and Raffaele. It was rewarding to see the slow but steady change in the media stories, and online blogs and comments. These were not comparable to actual court testimony, but the hope was if people everywhere could be made aware of the true facts, it could only help to eventually turn the tide. Watching the guilty verdicts overturned on live TV was amazing – I was so happy for Amanda and Raffaele and their families. What hell they must have gone through! It was hard enough just being involved in the online campaign to free them – the drama was unbelievable, and I can't imagine what it must have been like for the families. Yet I am so pleased that Amanda and Raffaele are free, and I hope that those of us who campaigned on their behalf had some role in that. I am very impressed by the people who built web sites, blogged, posted pictures, links, wrote articles, and posted counter arguments to the people who were illogically arguing for guilt. We were all accused of being paid shills in some PR campaign, but what really happened is that there was a small army of people who simply wanted to right a wrong, for no pay other than the satisfaction of doing the right thing.

They say, "The truth will set you free", and in this case, it has! Although what happened to Meredith Kercher will always be a tragedy, at least that tragedy is no longer made worse by unjustly imprisoning two of her friends.

komponisto

Although I have written about this case as an abstract lesson in human rationality (which it certainly is), and although being involved in it provided an opportunity to for me to exercise my foreign language skills, it was also about more than those things. It was about a couple of fine people -- Amanda and Raffaele -- whom I found to be worth caring about.

Everything I learned about Amanda from her family and friends -- and from Amanda herself when she spoke -- indicated strongly to me that she could easily have been a friend of mine, if only our paths had happened to cross. In fact I could empathize on some small scale with her predicament, since I too would no doubt have been considered "odd" by certain kinds of people. Like her, I am a devotee of languages and music; and, having once upon a time lived in the Seattle area myself, I feel an affinity with the open, adventurous culture of the Pacific Northwest . Over the past year and a half or so, I have had the opportunity to get to know Amanda through correspondence, which more than confirmed my impression that she is an intelligent, interesting, warm and caring person. I am proud to call her my friend.

Likewise, Raffaele is a person to whom I can relate in many ways; and every indication from anyone who has ever known him is that he is a high-quality individual and about as good a friend as you could ask for, not to mention being about the least likely person in the world to be involved in such a terrible crime. I could not stop thinking about how awful it must be to be Amanda or

Raffaele under these circumstances; and both of these people, I thought, deserved passionate advocacy from people beyond their immediate circle of family and friends. How could I "go on normally" while people like this were locked up in a cage? After all, if it had been me instead of them (as it could easily have been), I would certainly have hoped that at least someone out there would have felt similarly.

So, while my belief in Amanda and Raffaele's innocence follows strictly from impersonal reasoning about what the evidence implies, my "involvement" has had a large personal component. I genuinely like Amanda and Raffaele, and taking up their cause been a pleasure.

Jodie lee

I began supporting Amanda Knox and Raffaele Sollecito in 2007. I knew from the moment this began that these two kids were innocent. As a mother, my protective instincts took over for Amanda and Raffaele. I knew that I had to do something. I created a support group and began recruiting fellow supporters. When December, 2009 finally arrived, it felt like an eternity. I could only imagine how it must have felt for Amanda and Raffaele to be imprisoned for over two years, knowing they were innocent. When the verdict finally came, my heart broke for the kids and their families. I knew that we had to increase the awareness for their case. During this time I became a strong advocate and supporter. I spent days, weeks, and nights for the last four years, advocating for the truth to prevail. I had my children helping me through all of it and thinking of them as in Amanda and

Raffaele's place. I knew they were innocent since day one because the evidence didn't add up. I could see it in their hearts and faces that they were innocent and had nothing to do with it. I am very happy to have been able to help Amanda and Raffaele and I am delighted that they are finally free.

Jo Justus

I'm Jo Justus from Dayton Tenn, AKA on Facebook as: Jo Justus, AKA Grace More, AKA currently Jerry Morgan. I never use my real name on the interned due to being a victim of identity theft.

When I heard the guilty verdict I became very angry because I knew Amanda and Raffaele were innocent so I walked to my PC and began to research and do what ever I could to help prove their innocence. On Facebook I first hooked up with Jodie Leah who hooked me up with Bruce Fisher and our group grew to many people all dedicated to help free Amanda and Raffaele by informing the public and everyone of the truth/facts. This Facebook group consist of a great bunch of people and I'm proud to have been a part of it.

I'm a 62 y/o retired nuclear power plant operator / senior reactor operator. I spent 18 months researching all the info about this case that I could find (especially the motivation reports), gathering proof of their innocence and collecting the many lies the authorities presented in court and to the public. I presented this information to the public by posting on news articles and writing an article on ground report. I spent much of my time routing traffic from YouTube to Injustice In Perugia. Some people think I was obsessed because I devoted 18 months of my life to this effort but I like to think I was determined to see justice prevail for Amanda and Raffaele. I am thrilled that Amanda and Raffaele are free. If they had been found guilty I don't think I could handle the depression that this would have caused.

I worked hard for Amanda and Raffaele so fate delt me my just reward :(I was a motorcycle rider but will never get on one again. On Aug 28 th, 2011 a car turned cross my path forced me emergency stop causing me to lay the bike down and shattering my shin bone. I was in the hospital until Oct 5 2011 so I watched the verdict and Amanda's flight home at the hospital. It is nice to know that occasionally some things do work out right in this otherwise screwed up world.

I hope Amanda and Raffaele can drop in on Facebook and say hello to our FB group after they get rested up. All of us worked very hard for their freedom and it would mean a lot to us for them to say hello.

Tom Mininger
For a year and a half after the murder, I assumed that Amanda and Raffaele were guilty from the snippets I read in the media. Then I walked in on the end of a 48 hours episode my Mom was watching. I asked, "So… is she guilty?" expecting to get a yes. But Mom said no.

This made me curious so I dug into the case. I was horrified that after the havoc Mignini wreaked in the

Monster of Florence case, tormenting twenty innocent suspects plus journalists, he was allowed to embarrass his office again with another absurd group crime theory.

I also had enough science background to understand that the supposed physical evidence against Amanda and Raffaele was insubstantial even if it did exist, while the solid blood transfer and DNA evidence against the burglar was damning.

And where was the recording of Amanda's so called "confession" ?

I pledged to help these two kids. I found myself emotionally drained participating in the Perugia Shock comment sections. My niche became writing to the media, human rights groups and government persistently. I also donated many copies of "The Monster of Florence", "Murder In Italy", "Injustice In Perugia", and "The Monster of Perugia" to public and university libraries.

I shared the anguish of December 5, 2009 with many unknown friends, along with the high anxiety and eventual relief of October 3, 2011. I met The Innocence Project along the way, which I will support for life. And I am forever indebted to all my comrades who helped bring Amanda and Raffaele home to their wonderful families.

13

selfless sacrifice

As we have now seen, many sacrifices have been made by those most dedicated to helping Amanda and Raffaele secure their freedom. In this chapter I will highlight the personal sacrifice made by Steve Moore and his wife Michelle. Their dedication to the cause went far above and beyond all expectations and has truly been an inspiration to myself and others working to achieve the same goal.

Steve Moore is a retired FBI Agent who has 25 years of investigative experience. His experience includes the investigation and prosecution of violent crime, from murder to mass-murder and terrorism. Steve researched the Meredith Kercher murder case extensively and concluded that Amanda Knox and Raffaele Sollecito were innocent. Steve's expert opinion is one that must be respected when it comes to crimes of this nature. Steve has done invaluable work for Injustice in Perugia and has worked tirelessly to spread the truth about this case.

After a fulfilling career with the FBI, Steve was hired by Pepperdine University as the Deputy Director of Public Safety; his experience made the job a perfect fit. In his short time on the job Steve received good performance reviews for making several improvements to campus security.

With everything going well at work, Steve was shocked to find himself faced with a major decision in September 2010, when Pepperdine gave him an ultimatum; stop advocating for Amanda Knox or face termination.

This decision was not an easy one for Steve to make as he had a family to think about. There was a mortgage payment coming due and many other bills to pay. There was also the fact that two of his children were planning on going to Pepperdine, where they would have attended for greatly reduced tuition based on Steve's employment with the university.

After discussing the decision with his family, Steve informed the university that he would not be silenced. Steve was fired shortly thereafter for refusing to comply with Pepperdine's ill-planned ultimatum.

Steve discussed his firing with CBS Crimesider:

> *"Pepperdine gave me the option of staying," Steve Moore says, if he stopped talking about Amanda Knox. And Moore says, "If I had any doubts about her innocence, I would have stayed. But I don't."*

Steve's response to the University should be a lesson for all of us; honesty and integrity have far more value in our lives than anything money can bring.

Pepperdine is a Christian school with an enrollment of 7,000 students. The school's "Affirmation Statement" says, "That, truth, having nothing to fear from investigation, should be pursued relentlessly in every discipline". It appears that Pepperdine ignored their core beliefs when they decided to fire Steve Moore. Ironically, Steve was fired just weeks after Pepperdine students had organized a Free Speech Week on campus to commemorate the signing of the U.S. Constitution on September 17, 1787.

What was it that caused Steve to become involved with the Amanda Knox case in the first place? His life changing moment occurred when he accepted a challenge from his wife Michelle regarding the case. Michelle had watched a 48 Hours Mystery program about the case that convinced her Amanda had been railroaded. Steve spent 25 years putting bad guys in prison so it would take a lot more than a television show to convince him of a person's guilt or innocence. Knowing her husband well, Michelle challenged Steve to investigate the case and prove her wrong. Steve took his wife's challenge, conducted a thorough investigation, and to his surprise, he too concluded that Amanda Knox was innocent.

After Steve became active with IIP he explained why he felt he had an obligation to help Amanda Knox:

"I could not see this injustice and do nothing, any more than a doctor could see a person collapse and fail to render assistance, or a fireman hear the cries of children inside a burning house and stand idly by"

Steve's expert opinion would not go unnoticed leading to interviews with every major network in America and even a couple in the United Kingdom. His message was loud and clear; re-test the DNA evidence. As I mention several times in this book, the defense requested independent testing during the first trial but that request was denied, leaving the prosecution's expert as the final word. This was a crushing blow to the defense all but guaranteeing that Amanda and Raffaele would be convicted.

The entire case would come down to the DNA evidence and freedom for Amanda and Raffaele would never come if additional testing was not authorized. Steve's analysis told him that the DNA was faulty and he was not shy about telling the world what he had concluded. In fact Steve spent months telling anyone who would listen that an injustice had occurred in Perugia Italy.

We will never know to what extent outside pressure may have influenced Judge Hellmann's decision to appoint independent experts to take another look at the DNA on appeal, but one thing is certain, Steve's wish was granted. The DNA evidence that once condemned Amanda and Raffaele would have an opposite effect on appeal, all but guaranteeing freedom for the two.

Of course Steve's support of Amanda Knox did not sit well with the guilters, led by Peggy Ganong and Peter Quennell. One member of the group, SomeAlibi, vowed to "take down" Steve for simply believing Amanda was innocent, and the group encouraged all of their followers to write letters to Pepperdine in an attempt to get Steve fired. SomeAlibi openly admitted that he contacted Pepperdine in a post on an online forum:

> *"I contacted Pepperdine to provide with all of the online content of Steve Moore's interviews etc. to save them time. Since Steve stands by them I believe you couldn't object to that. I also pointed out the factual errors in them."*

Why is a group that claims to gather for Meredith Kercher contacting employers of anyone in attempt to adversely affect their employment? More importantly, why did Pepperdine listen? How could Steve's involvement with the Amanda Knox case have a negative impact on Pepperdine? One possibility was that Pepperdine had a campus in Florence, Italy. Did the university act after hearing complaints from the Italian campus?

Pepperdine's student newspaper *The Graphic* put any possible speculation to rest that Steve may have been causing a disruption for Pepperdine in Italy when it reported that the Florence campus was completely unaware of Steve's support of Amanda Knox, in fact the Florence campus had received no negative feedback from anyone in Italy regarding Steve Moore.

There is no doubt that the hate campaign against Steve Moore by the Quennell-Ganong cult influenced

Pepperdine's decision. The details will never be discussed publicly due to a legal agreement between Steve Moore and Pepperdine, but I will say that it is my opinion that Pepperdine hastily responded to the complaints coming from the Anti-Knox group and would have never thought to take action otherwise.

Upon hearing the news that Steve had been terminated, the Quennell-Ganong cult celebrated as if they had achieved great success. Unfortunately for them, their celebration was premature because when it was all said and done Steve Moore would be well compensated for his wrongful termination.

Steve filed a lawsuit shortly after he was fired; the preliminary judge reviewed the case and determined his complaint was valid, setting the trial date for August. Pepperdine moved for summary judgment, which was denied. It looked like Pepperdine had no interest in seeing the inside of a courtroom, offering a settlement instead. Steve discussed the settlement on his blog:

> *"I am happy to announce that Pepperdine and I have reached a satisfactory settlement of the lawsuit. As a stipulation requested by Pepperdine, I have agreed to keep the terms of the settlement confidential. But I can tell you that Michelle and I are happy with the settlement and we feel very much vindicated! I would like to thank the University for doing the right thing at this juncture. With the stress of that ordeal over, the family has plans to vacation in Maui later this summer."*

I have great respect for Steve and Michelle Moore and I was very pleased that Pepperdine chose to do what was right in the end. Steve and Michelle have sacrificed greatly for a cause they believe in and I am honored to call them friends.

14

who's accusing who?

Would the outcome of the first trial ended differently if there had not been a civil trial running concurrently with the murder trial? Unfortunately, that is a question that will forever remain unanswered but it certainly warrants speculation.

There were two civil suits running concurrently with the murder trial. Both would be damaging but one of the lawsuits would carry more weight than the other. The

Kercher family filed a lawsuit against whoever was proven guilty of murdering Meredith. Italy allows civil suits to be filed in advance of the outcome of the actual murder trial, a practice not seen in the United States. This is common practice in Italy so the Kerchers were simply following protocol.

The second lawsuit was filed by Patrick Lumumba against Amanda Knox for defamation. This lawsuit would prove to be extremely damaging to Amanda as it certainly influenced the murder trial. Lumumba wanted compensation because Amanda "accused" him of murdering Meredith. Early on, Lumumba had told the press that he was mistreated by the police and endured a brutal interrogation. You would think that his experience with the police would give him an understanding as to why Amanda described a "vision" during her interrogation that imagined Lumumba attacking Meredith while Amanda listened from another room (I discuss Amanda's interrogation extensively in "Injustice in Perugia" and again in the Preface of this book). As we know, Amanda endured an all night interrogation where she was repeatedly told that Lumumba committed the crime and she was told to imagine that it occurred. Shortly after the interrogation ended, Amanda recanted her statements stating that she was under the pressures of stress, shock and extreme exhaustion. Amanda's retraction had no influence on the police; they needed their trio of suspects to fulfill Mignini's fantasy so they rushed out to arrest Lumumba anyway.

The ordeal began for Lumumba and his family in the early morning hours of November 6, 2007, when he and his wife Aleksandra were shocked out of bed by the doorbell ringing, followed by up to twenty police officers barging through their door. Lumumba was forcefully taken from his home as his wife tried to console their screaming son, Davide. Lumumba would later recall the event during interviews:

> *"They were wearing normal clothes and carrying guns, I thought it must be some sort of armed gang about to kill me. I was terrified."*

> *"They hit me over the head and yelled 'dirty black'. Then they put handcuffs on me and shoved me out of the door, as Aleksandra pulled Davide away, screaming."*

The police were well prepared when they came for Lumumba, bringing a fleet of seven squad cars to his home in order to give him a safe escort him back to the police station. When Lumumba arrived at the station, much like Amanda, he was subjected to a long grueling interrogation.

Lumumba revealed this information in an interview with the Daily Mail. I certainly do not view the Daily Mail as a reliable source but Lumumba later confirmed everything with Katie Crouch from Slate.com.

> *"I was questioned by five men and women, some of whom punched and kicked me. They forced me on my knees against the wall and said I should be in America where I would be given the electric chair for my crime. All they kept saying was, 'You did it, you did it.'"*

"I didn't know what I'd 'done'. I was scared and humiliated. Then, after a couple of hours one of them suggested they show me a picture of 'the dead girl' to get me to confess.

"It might sound naive, but it was only then that I made the connection between Meredith's death and my arrest. Stunned, I said, You think I killed Meredith?"

Lumumba spent two weeks in prison before being released because he had a rock solid alibi. Lumumba repeatedly told police that he was at his bar Le Chic at the time of the murder. Thankfully for him, a Swiss professor that had spent the evening in question at Le Chic talking to Lumumba came forward to confirm Lumumba's whereabouts. Without this alibi, Lumumba could have easily spent a year in jail (like Amanda and Raffaele) waiting to see if the police decided to press charges.

At some point after his release, Lumumba decided to change his story about his ordeal with the police. It seems that money certainly played a major role in his decision making. Lumumba sued the police for his wrongful imprisonment seeking 516,000 Euros (approx. $700,000) in damages, but in the end he was only awarded $8,000.

If Lumumba wanted a higher payday he would have to pursue a case against Amanda Knox. He obviously could not stick with his story that he was horribly mistreated by the police if he expected to win a lawsuit against Amanda because his claims would further support Amanda's defense argument that her statements were coerced. So, without explanation, Lumumba changed his story. Now Lumumba would claim that he was not beaten by his interrogators and called a stupid black. In fact he decided to buddy up with the same police officers that he had once accused of mistreatment, acting as if they were exemplary officers just doing their jobs.

There is no doubt that Lumumba's claims were helpful to the prosecution in the murder trial. Lumumba was now praising the police publicly while demonizing Amanda Knox every time he had the opportunity. Lumumba was first to make the claim that Amanda was jealous of Meredith. His claims were obviously fabricated because he barely knew Amanda. Lumumba had never visited Amanda's home and had rarely interacted with Amanda and Meredith at anytime outside of the bar, yet he somehow knew that tensions were high at the cottage and that Amanda had jealousy issues.

Lumumba also claimed that he fired Amanda for flirting with customers. This claim once again helped Mignini to paint Amanda in a bad light. The truth is that Lumumba never fired Amanda. She was still waiting tables and handing out flyers for Le Chic on a part time basis on the days leading up to the murder. We know that Lumumba texted Amanda on the night of the murder to let her know that she was not needed at work. Why would this text be necessary if Lumumba had already fired her? It is pretty obvious that Lumumba was attempting to smear Amanda in any way that he could. This time he was caught in a lie. Lumumba's claims were a gift for the prosecution and Mignini did not hesitate to take every negative detail about Amanda and run with it.

Lumumba has spent the past four years defaming Amanda in the press and continues to do so even now that Amanda has been declared innocent and released. As recently as October 31, 2011, Lumumba repeated the lie that Amanda has never shown any concern for his plight and he repeated that he believes that Amanda was responsible for Meredith's death. His opinion has changed very little since making this angry statement right after his release:

> *"She was angry I was firing her and wanted revenge," he says. "By the end, she hated me. But I don't even think she's evil. To be evil you have to have a soul. Amanda doesn't. She's empty; dead inside. She's the ultimate actress, able to switch her emotions on and off in an instant. I don't believe a word she says. Everything that comes out of her mouth is a lie. But those lies have stained me forever."*

The news often repeats Lumumba's claims that Amanda has never apologized to Lumumba for his ordeal. The truth is that Amanda does not owe Lumumba an apology, the police do. With that said, Amanda being the kind hearted person that she is, stated on two separate occasions that she felt horrible about what happened to Lumumba and that she was sorry that he was put through hell.

Lumumba's attorney, Carlo Pascelli, has been one of the vilest attackers of Amanda Knox. It is clear that Pascelli is bitter that the compensation was low for Lumumba's confinement, leading him to seek out other avenues for cash. Amanda was an easy target for Pascelli. During court hearings he describes Amanda as a diabolical she-devil.

So the question remains, would the outcome of the first trial gone differently if Lumumba did not seek damages from Amanda Knox? If the civil suit had not been filed, the court would have not heard anything about the statements that Amanda's signed during her interrogation. No information whatsoever about accusing an innocent man would have been presented to the jury. The Italian Supreme Court ruled that the information acquired during the interrogation was inadmissible in the murder trial, stating that the interrogation was illegal because Amanda did not have an attorney present. Because the civil trial ran concurrently, the jury heard the damaging details anyway.

Add the fact that the civil trial gave Carlo Pascelli several opportunities to smear Amanda in court, telling the jury that she was an actress crying crocodile tears. There is no doubt that this was damaging to Amanda. Were the statements showing Amanda accusing an innocent man, along with the vicious attacks on Amanda's character made by Pascelli, enough to sway the jury to believe in guilt?

I cannot say for sure if Lumumba's actions caused the wrongful convictions but I can say that Lumumba's behavior has been reprehensible. He knows how the system in Perugia works. He was taken out of his home in the middle of the night and beaten by the same police force that he has now befriended, all in the pursuit of money. I honestly do not know how Lumumba sleeps at night knowing what he has done.

15

irreparable damage

We as a people are always trying to fix the things in life that are broken and right the things that are wrong. Unfortunately some things in life are not repairable. In fact some things are so horribly wrong that nothing will ever make them right. Unfortunately this is the case with Meredith Kercher and anyone else on this earth that has had their lives stolen from them by acts of pure evil.

In the case of Meredith Kercher, nothing can ever make it right. Her life was stolen from her in an act of senseless violence. Her family will forever be left with the sorrow of her loss and no real closure will ever come. I realize this is a blunt assessment but it is based on the reality of knowing how strong a parent's love is for their children.

For the Kercher's the tragedy they have suffered has been compounded by the authorities that handled the case. Finding justice for Meredith may have never brought closure but it could have helped greatly as the family struggled to cope with their loss. Unfortunately, just as closure will always be out of reach, justice will never come for Meredith. This was guaranteed when two innocent people were convicted for her murder.

On December 4, 2009, when Amanda and Raffaele were wrongfully convicted, the case stopped being about Meredith Kercher. Wrongful convictions cause insufferable damage to all involved. The additional suffering the Kerchers have been forced to endure is not the fault of Amanda and Raffaele. They along with the Kerchers are being wrongly punished due to the negligence of the authorities in Perugia, Italy.

I cannot imagine the pain felt by Meredith's family to have this ordeal dragged out for as long as it has, but I do know that the pain the Kerchers are forced to live with everyday will never be a legitimate excuse to destroy the lives of two innocent people.

I have been writing about this case for nearly two years and I have never been able to bring myself to write about the Kercher's active involvement in this case and it pains me to do so here. My wife and I have three amazing children and I cannot even bear to think about something horrible happening to any of them let alone trying to imagine trying to deal with the situation if it occurred. I do not wish to criticize the Kerchers in anyway but I do feel that the Kerchers have opened the door for discussion by the public statements they have made.

The Kerchers have been praised throughout the course of the trial for their silence and respect for the Italian legal process, but the truth is they have been far from silent. John Kercher is a tabloid writer that has consistently written articles that have been purposefully timed to have an influence on the appeal trial.

The first article was well placed right in between the November 24 appeal start date and the December 11 hearing where Amanda gave an emotional statement to the court, during which the Kercher's attorney, Francesco Maresca, walked out while Amanda was speaking.

December 2, 2010: *"It's utterly despicable that the girl jailed for killing my daughter has become a celebrity"*

The second article was released on December 18, the day Judge Hellmann granted the independent DNA review.

December 18, 2010: *"We will never forget our murdered daughter Meredith Kercher"*

The third article came the day after the March 12 court date where bus drivers gave testimony discrediting the prosecution's star witness Antonio Curatolo.

March 13, 2011: *"Rescuing Meredith from the 'Foxy Knoxy' frenzy"*

The fourth article was printed on the original date the DNA report was suppose to be reviewed. As it turned out, the independent experts requested additional time so this article missed the mark.

May 21, 2011: *"My View"*

Just before the appeal was to resume after the summer recess the Kercher family would once again speak out. This time it was Meredith's sister, Stephanie Kercher that opened up for the first time in an open letter to Francesco Maresca which was in turn leaked to the press. In the letter Stephanie asks Maresca "Please don't let Meredith's death be in vain." She also asked that the focus be put on her sister rather that the evidence:

> *"The defence seem to be focusing on these DNA aspects but we want, for a moment to remember who this case is about: My sister, a daughter brutally taken away four years ago, and a day does not pass when we do not think about her and can bring this to an end"*

I do not know if the Kerchers have been influenced by their attorney, Francesco Maresca, or if their feelings are uninfluenced heartfelt emotions, but either way, their feelings should have had absolutely no influence on the appeal. Stephanie's emotional pleas to remember Meredith instead of focusing on facts were a clear sign that Justice must be blind. Emotion cannot be allowed to dictate the outcome of a trial. Steve Moore explains this far better than I ever could:

> *"Justice is blind for a reason. Only in the penalty phases can the pain and grief of the family be taken*

into account. A trial is not about retribution. A trial is about the finding of facts. Emotion is corrosive to facts. Mixing emotion with fact degrades fact, not emotion. If emotions are allowed to influence fact in a trial, all is lost. And this is the reason that the involvement of victims' families are always against their own best interests."

There is no doubt that the Kercher's attorney, Francesco Maresca, believes that Amanda and Raffaele are guilty as he has rubber stamped the prosecution's case at every turn. He represents the Kerchers in the civil aspect of the case, making it his job to secure a monetary settlement for the Kercher family. Maresca has represented the Kerchers at most of the hearings leaving observers to assume that he reports back the details of each hearing to his clients. The Kerchers were not present during most of the first trial, flying in only to hear the verdict. I do not blame the Kerchers for not attending the trial, I am not sure I would be able to sit through the nightmare myself. The only relevance to their absence is the fact that they relied on their attorney for information.

Maresca has made no effort to hide his disdain for Amanda Knox. As previously mentioned, when Amanda spoke to the court at the beginning of the appeal, Maresca walked out of the courtroom while she was speaking. My heart tells me that Maresca has guided the Kerchers public statements but I have nothing more to prove that point. Stephanie's open letter to Maresca that was instantly turned over to the press is another reason for this belief.

One would have to believe that Maresca would have the best interests of his clients at heart regardless of how he felt about the case. This made Maresca's presentation during closing arguments even that much more shocking. In an act absent of any decency or respect toward the clients that he represents, Maresca, without warning, displayed photographs of Meredith's body in open court, simply for shock value. Steve Moore was in court when the photos were presented and made these observations:

"without warning, without dignity, without any apparent concern for Meredith or her grieving family, without decency, an attorney began to display eight foot square, gruesome, lurid and obscene naked full-frontal photographs of Meredith Kercher's blood-smeared body, lying on the floor next to her bed where she had been murdered and sexually assaulted. She lay in the very position that Rudy Guede left her after putting a pillow under her hips to assist in the sexual assault. The photos were, to say the least, explicit, and press cameras immediately began clicking, as the courtroom spectators stood and moved toward the huge screen where the large photos were being displayed. Meredith was shown from the tips of her toes all the way to her eyes, fixed in a glassy, gruesome stare above a gaping throat slash. The audience gasped. More grisly photos followed; close-ups of the deep slash to Meredith's throat, showing the severed muscles and larynx. But still the photos continued; photos which showed graphically the sputum foam which was the result of her labored breathing as the blood from her neck drained into her lungs. The photos showed her empty eyes and her blood-caked hair."

"The graphic, obscene, desecrating photographs shown today had no evidentiary value. No legitimate purpose was served by the photographs. Nothing about the murder scene was in dispute in this session. Nothing about Meredith's death, her condition at the time of death, or her body was in play. In short, there was no reason in the entire legal world to show detailed photographs of the violated body of his clients' child and sister. No reason except money. The display was gratuitous, designed to horrify and shock a jury. And it horrified. And it shocked. But maybe only the conscience of decent people. Several people left the courtroom, and many were left traumatized."

Maresca's actions showed one thing, he cared more about money than he did about Meredith Kercher. Maresca represented the Kerchers with regard to the civil suit against Amanda and Raffaele. Victory for Maresca meant cash in his pocket and nothing else. Throughout the entire first trial and the appeal, the courtroom was closed to all outsiders whenever it was necessary to show Meredith's body during criminal proceedings, a gruesome reality that is unavoidable in a murder trial. Maresca chose to put Meredith on display without any warning whatsoever, in a courtroom overflowing with camera ready journalists, in an attempt to secure a monetary settlement. I find myself at a loss for appropriate words to describe my disgust for Maresca's malicious behavior.

In her open letter that made its way to the press, Stephanie Kercher said, "We will continue our fight with the support of our lawyer, Francesco Maresca." I have to wonder if the Kerchers still had the same faith in Maresca after he pulled that repulsive stunt. Maresca later admitted that he did not have the Kercher's permission to show the photos but at the time of this writing, the Kerchers had yet to speak publicly on the matter.

Shortly after Amanda and Raffaele were declared innocent, Stephanie Kercher spoke out once again asking that Meredith remain the focus. She requested that people use a picture of her sister Meredith as their profile picture on social media sites to help balance the news coverage so that Meredith would not be forgotten.

The truth is Meredith Kercher has not been forgotten. In fact her name has remained in the news for the past four years for very unfortunate reasons. If the murder investigation had been handled properly, her killer, Rudy Guede, would have been in custody very early on and the world may have never heard of Meredith Kercher, because there would have been no lurid details to entice the press. If Amanda and Raffaele had not been wrongfully accused, and the sex game gone wrong fantasy had never been told by the authorities, Meredith's case would have sadly been just one of the many other unfortunate murders that have occurred in the world.

I am hopeful that the day will come that the Kercher family will see that they were horribly betrayed by their attorney and the authorities in Perugia, Italy. I am hopeful they will eventually see the truth and begin to find some kind of peace.

16

last act for prosecution and closing arguments

When court resumed on September 5 2011 (day 1400), the prosecution showed that they had no intention of giving up, even though their case had suffered a huge blow from the Conti and Vecchiotti report that was presented to the court just before summer recess.

Just prior to the summer break, scrambling to recover from Conti and Vecchiotti's scathing report, the prosecution requested additional time to question the independent experts, and Francesco Maresca, the attorney representing the Kercher family decided that he had more questions as well. Patrizia Stefanoni's reputation was shredded by Conti and Vecchiotti so it was no surprise when she requested the opportunity to defend herself on the stand. All requests were granted by Judge Hellmann and would be the first orders of business as the trial resumed after summer break.

Conti and Vecchiotti returned to court to take on another barrage of questions from Francesco Maresca. Maresca gave it his best shot but had absolutely no success in tarnishing the work of Conti and Vecchiotti. In fact the questions actually helped to reinforce their conclusions. Maresca kept hammering away at the bra clasp evidence, insisting that Raffaele's DNA must have been present. When Maresca questioned why one of the tests conducted by Conti and Vecchiotti only showed partially completed results, he received a decisive response that demolished his position. Vecchiotti explained to the court;

> *"After examining just the first 4 markers out of 17, there were already new alleles for forming at least eight profiles so there was no need to continue to find the all of them. In fact, There were so many alleles that even my own profile was a match in 9 markers"* *Vecchiotti then looked at Judge Hellmann, "Your own profile, President, could likely be found in that DNA."*

Patrizia Stefanoni was next to take the stand in what would end up being a failed attempt to defend her work. Stefanoni proceeded to tell the court that her procedures were just fine regardless what anyone else thought. She decided to use plastic collection bags and, according to her that was fine. She admitted to storing evidence in the freezer of the cottage, once again, no problem. When questioned about missing data, she replied "I forgot." No mistakes were made; she just forgot to record a few things, no big deal. According to Stefanoni, no contamination occurred and she claimed her work was completely acceptable. At the end of the day, Stefanoni may have been the only person on earth that still held onto those beliefs.

On September 7 2011 (day 1402) Prosecutor Comodi would take center stage, taking one more shot at Conti and Vecchiotti's armor, by asking the court for new independent experts and new tests to be performed on the knife because Conti and Vecchiotti got it all wrong.

After doing everything in their power to block any additional testing during the first trial, now it was the prosecution asking for additional testing. After everything that had transpired, it seemed completely unreasonable to ask for more tests. The DNA was tested by the prosecution's experts during the first trial and then by court appointed experts during the second trial. It was clear that no additional tests were needed. The request was just a ploy to keep Amanda and Raffaele in prison for a longer period of time. Thankfully Judge Hellmann was not moved by Comodi's performance, denying the request, giving great satisfaction to the defense and bringing Amanda and Raffaele one step closer to freedom. The prosecution's request was the last order of business, leading Judge Hellmann to schedule closing arguments to begin on September 23 2011.

Closing Arguments

"I couldn't believe the things I was hearing, everything started over as if we were still in November 2007, as if Amanda and Raffaele had just been arrested, as if in 4 years nobody had been working at this case at all."
—Frank Sfarzo, Perugia Shock

On September 23, 2011 (day 1418), as the closing arguments began, Injustice in Perugia was fortunate to have live updates coming from sources inside the courtroom. This was a very difficult time for Amanda and Raffaele as they would once again be subjected to horrible accusations and outright lies from a group that was hell-bent on destroying them.

Lead Prosecutor Giancarlo Costagliola was the first to take the stage during closing arguments. Costagliola was overshadowed throughout the appeal by Prosecutors Mignini and Comodi, who were retained as assistant counsel from the first trial. This was Costagliola's chance to shine but unfortunately for him, his performance was rather dull and far less than convincing.

Costagliola stood before the court and repeated the same tired lines that we heard throughout the first trial as if nothing at all had even been discussed on appeal. The disco busses that were proven nonexistent appeared again in his speech, attempting to restore the credibility of Antonio Curatolo. Costagliola completely ignored Curatolo's embarrassing testimony where he claimed to be using heroin on the night he allegedly witnessed activity outside the location of the murder. Did Costagliola forget that Curatolo's testimony was cut short by the judge, as he ordered Curatolo to be removed from the courtroom immediately?

No, Costagliola did not forget Curatolo's pitiful performance; he decided to defend Curatolo instead, attempting to claim that heroin does not cause hallucinations so Curatolo's testimony must be considered reliable. This claim is ridiculous of course but it worked during the first trial so I guess that Costagliola figured, why not try it again?

If defending Curatolo was not shocking enough, Costagliola proceeded to bring up another de-bunked accusation by telling the court that Raffaele called the Carabinieri (Italian police) after the postal police arrived, even though it had already been proven in court that Raffaele made the call much earlier (as previously discussed in the Lifetime chapter). It was mind boggling to hear updates coming from the courtroom that the same arguments were being made all over again as if it was still 2007.

Costagliola concluded his performance by informing the court that the media was responsible for the major turn of events in the case. Costagliola ordered that the media must not be allowed to influence the verdict, saying that Amanda and Raffaele had been recently portrayed in a good light. He went further to suggest that the court should rule on emotion rather than facts, by asking the court to think about Meredith's family:

"There has been an obsessive campaign, in particular by Italian newspapers and TV, which has given a voice to the parents of Amanda & Raffaele, two young people from good families held in prison by the obstinacy of the Prosecution. I hope on the other

*hand that in deciding you will listen a little to the
parents of Meredith."*

Costagliola's comments were absurd, completely
ignoring the enormous effect the media had on the
outcome of the first trial, but paled in comparison to the
egregious exaggerations the court would soon hear from
Giuliano Mignini.

When it was Mignini's time to take the stage, the
public was asked to leave the courtroom which meant
only one thing; Mignini would once again attempt to
influence the jury with gruesome crime scene and
autopsy photographs. As the photographs flashed on the
big screen, Mignini complained of "Nazi-like tactics"
used by the defense to discredit police experts causing
Meredith Kercher to be forgotten. The truth is Mignini
told the court what they already knew, Meredith Kercher
was brutally murdered. Showing her body provided no
proof as to who killed her. Mignini's ploy certainly did
nothing to show that Amanda and Raffaele were guilty
and in my opinion was disrespectful to Meredith.

During the first trial, Mignini cherished his time on
stage, rambling on for over seven hours, barking out de-
bunked myths, misinformation and outright lies. As it
turned out, this veteran performer felt little need to work
on his act for the appeal, taking the stage once again to
repeat the same tired lines, with a few additional
exaggerations thrown in from time to time.

In Mignini's world, his witnesses were still credible.
Mignini defended Antonio Curatolo's testimony, saying
that it must not be overlooked, never mind the heroin.
Mignini suggested that Marco Quintavalle, the store
owner that claimed to see Amanda, was still credible,

even though he had the color of Amanda's coat wrong and his own employee discredited him. I know the coat color may not seem like a big deal, but when you look at the big picture, it completely demolishes the witness. The truth is Quintavalle saw Amanda on the news wearing a gray coat so when he described Amanda, he said her coat was gray. Unfortunately for Quintavalle, Amanda was seen on the news wearing Raffaele's gray coat. Amanda's coat is actually blue. Mignini suggested that Quintavalle saw Amanda's black and white striped sweatshirt under her coat and he put the two colors together in his mind creating gray. Mignini's ridiculous explanation did little to revive his de-bunked witness.

Mignini took Costagliola's comments about the media's role to new heights by telling the court that Amanda's PR efforts cost her family eleven million dollars. For years, the public heard lies about the PR firm coming with a price tag of one million dollars, Mignini somehow managed to add ten million dollars to the lie.

Mignini spent twenty minutes telling the court not to listen to the support groups for Amanda and Raffaele. Without mentioning anyone by name, Mignini went on to describe Steve Moore and the websites for IIP and FOA, telling the court that we were not to be trusted. The truth is if he did not think we made a major impact he would have never mentioned us in the first place.

Mignini proceeded to stumble through many of the same vindictive talking points that he bellowed out at the first trial, as if nothing had changed, completely ignoring everything presented on appeal. I discuss Mignini's theories in great detail in "Injustice in Perugia" so, unlike Mignini, I will not recycle that material here.

Manuela Comodi was next to take the stage, and once again she did her best to defend the work of Patrizia Stefanoni in an attempt to discredit the work of Conti and Vecchiotti; once again failing to make her case. Comodi spoke most of the day, going through her script from the first trial point by point as if Conti and Vecchiotti had not already discredited her. Giuliano Mignini was so bored with her presentation that he actually fell asleep in the courtroom.

Having the civil suits running concurrently with the murder trial meant that Amanda and Raffaele would have to endure another barrage of insults from civil attorneys Francesco Maresca and Carlo Pascelli during closing arguments.

These two attorneys were vicious throughout both trials. Amanda sat there once again listening to Pascelli rant on that she was a "diabolical she-devil", a woman "without a soul." Then came the incident that I detailed in the previous chapter regarding Francesco Maresca's repulsive stunt, when he took Mignini's ploy of showing photos of Meredith one step further, by flashing her naked body up on the video screen without warning. At least Mignini had the courtesy to clear the public from the courtroom, not Maresca; he was going for pure shock value. Thankfully, in the end, the theatrics of Pascelli and Maresca would not work in their favor.

Finally, the prosecution ended its closing arguments, requesting that the court increase the sentence for Amanda and Raffaele. For Amanda, they wanted life in prison with six months in solitary confinement as additional punishment. For Raffaele, they wanted life in jail with two months of solitary confinement as additional punishment. Even as their case crumbled before them, their vindictive nature continued to be on display.

The prosecution failed to realize that the outcome of the appeal rested solely on the evidence that Judge Hellmann highlighted at the beginning of the appeal. Hellmann was very clear as to what he felt needed to be looked at, knowing that no other evidence carried enough weight to secure a conviction; yet the prosecution insisted on rehashing old arguments that had no relevance at all.

The Defense Speaks
On September 27, 2011 (day 1422), Raffaele's attorneys were the first to speak. Raffaele's attorney Giulia Buongiorno informed the court that the defense would only focus on the facts with no unnecessary theatrics. Buongiorno addressed the prosecution's claims that the media was improperly influencing the appeal, reminding the court that the media was horrible to Amanda and Raffaele the first time around. The negative headlines have far outweighed the positive ones, making it quite interesting for the prosecution to be critical at this point. The shift in the media during the appeal was not influenced by anything other than the actual facts of the case. Buongiorno then called out Mignini's attempt to sway the jury with photos of Meredith, saying that the photos did nothing more than to cause a distraction and did nothing to show guilt.

Raffaele's attorneys often found themselves defending Amanda instead of Raffaele because the prosecution's case that put their client behind bars was centered on Amanda. During closing arguments Buongiorno would defend Amanda once again.

Buongiorno told the court that the case became a soap opera and Amanda was the main character. The police went looking for any details they could find about Amanda to add to their story. Looking for ex-boyfriends to build a story about her sex life and using the most incriminating photos they could find. The photo of Amanda and Raffaele kissing outside the cottage had a huge impact on the case. Amanda was the focus with Raffaele only receiving mention as her boyfriend.

Buongiorno told the court that the prosecution created a fictional character that used her beauty to control men with the power of sex, comparing Amanda to Jessica Rabbit, a character from "Who killed Roger Rabbit." Buongiorno told the court that the prosecution described Amanda as a whore but in reality she is a faithful and loving friend stating; "Yes sometimes prosecutors make mistakes, but they should stop and fix them."

As promised, Buongiorno stuck with the facts of the case, hammering home the fact that there was no physical trace of Amanda or Raffaele in the room where Meredith was killed. She reinforced the fact that all of the evidence in the murder room pointed to Rudy Guede, telling the court that evidence showing that Guede was in the room shows that "no one could enter that room and not leave any trace."

Buongiorno also attacked the interrogation methods used against Amanda, saying she was interrogated by "hostile" officers, which made it impossible to trust any information collected during the interrogation. She went on to highlight the DNA analysis of Conti and Vecchiotti that shredded the prosecution's case. When it was all said and done, the court appointed independent experts would be the deciding factor.

Buongiorno concluded her closing arguments by asking the jury to keep her client in mind when making their decision: "The lives of this kid and his parents have been destroyed. You must today evaluate if - if - if these kids committed the crime."

Raffaele's attorney Luca Maori had the attention of the court during his closing arguments when he presented some very interesting data. As discussed in great detail throughout the course of the first trial, Amanda's interrogation should have been recorded as required by law. Within 24 hours after the discovery of the murder, police were recording every cell phone call made by Amanda and Raffaele. Giuliano Mignini stated that he recorded the statements made by Amanda's flat mates and other witnesses. After Amanda was arrested, her phone calls from prison were also recorded. Italian law requires that recordings be made of interrogations once a suspect is detained. Amanda was a suspect when she signed the final statement on November 6, 2007, yet the police have no recording. Mignini first claimed it was an oversight but later suggested that there was simply a lack of funds to pay for such a recording.

The data that Maori presented to the court made Mignini's excuse look silly. Maori told the court that there have been 39,952 wiretapped calls throughout the course of the trial. This is a shocking figure that no doubt came at a huge expense. Maori explained that every single call is listened to by a live operator who has the task of taking notes detailing each call.

The notes taken for these calls provided disturbing information about the police. It appears that the operators spent most of their time insulting those they were listening too, calling family members of the accused names such as "pieces of shit" and "vipers."

The police had the resources to wiretap 39,952 calls but lacked the funds to record an interrogation; a recording that could have very well prevented this nightmare from ever occurring in the first place. It sounds like Mignini needs to come up with another excuse for not recording the interrogation.

On September 29, 2011 (day 1424), Attorney Carlo Dalla Vedova was the first to speak for Amanda Knox. Amanda's defense team had the same philosophy as Raffaele's; no theatrics, just the facts. Dalla Vedova reiterated to the court that investigators were hasty in their conclusions leading to the wrongful convictions. Dalla Vedova told the court that Amanda underwent a very grave violation of her rights. There was no reason to suspect Amanda in the days following the murder; nothing emerged from the wiretapping, and there was no evidence at the crime scene, nothing at all.

Along with the complete lack of evidence, Amanda also had an alibi; exactly the same alibi that her housemate Filomena had. Both Amanda and Filomena were at their boyfriend's houses and their boyfriends provided alibis.

Dalla Vedova went on to maintain that Conti and Vecchiotti had demolished the prosecution's case. "Today there's very little left," Dalla Vedova said. "A clue is not enough."

Dalla Vedova urged the court not to be afraid to recognize that the lower court made a mistake. "That's exactly why we have appeals—courts can make mistakes," he said. "Nobody is infallible."

Attorney Luciano Ghirga was next to speak for Amanda, telling the court that Amanda was "very afraid but her heart is full of hope and she hopes to return to freedom."

Ghirga told the court that Amanda's "image was massacred" by the media and the attacks on her character started before the first trial ever began. Every word Amanda spoke made its way into the headlines the very next day, but not before the media had a chance to twist the meaning of her words.

Ghirga has often been emotional in his defense of Amanda and he became emotional once again during his closing arguments when he told the court that he thought of Amanda like a daughter. He appealed to the jury to put themselves in the shoes of Amanda's family, countering prosecutor Costagliola's pleas for the jury to put themselves in the shoes of the Kercher family. Ghirga stressed that Amanda's family has never been part of any conspiracy to put pressure on the Italian courts to release their daughter, "they are parents and they deserve respect."

As closing arguments came to a close, the court would hear rebuttals from the prosecution, allowing the prosecution's key players to take the stage one last time, prolonging the nightmare for Amanda and Raffaele. Once again, both would be forced to sit in silence listening to hurtful accusations and vindictive lies.

Thankfully, after the rebuttals, both Amanda and Raffaele would be given the opportunity to address the court before the jury would convene to decide their fate. The rebuttals took place on Friday September 30, leading Judge Hellmann to schedule Amanda and Raffaele's statements for Monday October 3. I was told that he did not want the verdict read on a Saturday night as it would cause too much commotion in the college town. Unfortunately it meant that Amanda and Raffaele would be left to wait through what I am sure was a long agonizing weekend.

17

freedom

On October 3, 2011 (day 1427), Amanda Knox and
Raffaele Sollecito stood before the court and pleaded for
their lives. For me, it was infuriating to see two innocent
people being forced to beg for their freedom, after
already having nearly four years stolen from them. Both
had been courageous throughout both trials and would
somehow find a way to muster up enough strength in
order to stand strong while giving emotional speeches to
the court.

Raffaele was the first to speak. Here is an excerpt from his speech translated into English:

> *"I never hurt anyone, never in my whole life. The charge against me, it was so outlandish that I thought that it could disappear within a little amount of time, everything could be clarified. But this did not happen and somehow I had to endure and go on day by day and I've been living a nightmare."*

> *"On this bracelet is written 'Free Amanda and Raffaele.' It's a bracelet that I've have never taken off after I received it as a present. I think is time for me to take it off. It's a companion that gives me different emotions. There is a desire for justice. The efforts of the path I've taken in this dark tunnel. There is also the desire for freedom. And there is also the affection and the tenderness which we've shown each other ever since we've met. This bracelet is part of history and our past, it represents somehow the past. I hope it will bring new hopes in new future."*

The bracelet that Raffaele talks about can be viewed on the cover of this book. There is significant meaning in that bracelet, as it not only gave Raffaele hope but it also showed that he and Amanda would forever stand side by side in defense of their freedom. This unified stand was a bold symbol of innocence that should not have been ignored in Perugia, Italy.

When it was Amanda's turn to speak, she did an amazing job of keeping her composure as she stood before the court, often fighting back her tears, to deliver her emotional plea in fluent Italian.

Here is her speech translated into English:

"Members of the court. Many times people have said I am some other person, people don't understand whom I am. The only thing different from four years ago is what I have suffered. I lost a friend, a girlfriend, in the most brutal way in the most unexplained manner.

My trust in the police authorities has been betrayed. I have had to dealt with unfair and unfounded charges. I have paid with my life for things that I did not commit.

Four years ago I did not know what tragedy was. I have never faced so much anger before. I didn't know how to interpret it. How did we react when we found out Meredith had been killed? I did not believe it. How was it possible?

Her bedroom was next to mine. She was killed in our home. If I had been there that night I would have died. The only difference is, I was not there. I trusted the police's sense of duty and trust. I trusted them completely. I was betrayed on the night of November 5. I was manipulated.

I am not who they say I am. I am not violent. I don't have a lack of respect for life. And I did not kill. I did not rape. I did not steal. I wasn't there at the crime scene.

I had good relationships with everyone who lived in my flat. We all had good relationships. We helped each other. I shared my life, particularly with

Meredith. We were friends. She was worried about me. She was very kind to me.

I have never run away from the truth. I insist after four desperate years, that our innocence is true and needs to be recognized. I want to go back home. I want to go back to my life. I don't want my life and my future taken away from me for something that I didn't do.

I am innocent. We do not deserve this. We never did anything to deserve this. I have the utmost respect to this court and the care that it has shown. Thank you."

When Amanda finished speaking, her and Raffaele were escorted back to prison to wait for the jury to decide their fate. As the media swarmed in on Perugia Italy, and the world looked on, Amanda and Raffaele would once again be forced to wait. Judge Hellmann called in food for the jury but made no sleeping arrangements, meaning that a decision would most likely come before nightfall.

Later that evening, Amanda and Raffaele were escorted back into court to hear Judge Hellmann read the verdicts. I was surprised at how quickly it all developed as the scene appeared a little chaotic, with the language barrier also causing some confusion. When Hellmann began to speak, I heard the word "guilty," and for a moment I began to relive December 4, 2009, but we would quickly find out that Hellmann was not referring to the murder charge; he was referring to the charge of slander against Patrick Lumumba. Thankfully, Hellmann was speaking quickly so there was not a lot of time for anger to set in, as Hellmann's words would soon cause cheers throughout the courtroom. Amanda and Raffaele were free!

Just after the verdict was read, Amanda collapsed in tears, looking as if she needed support in order to stay on her feet, with what appeared to be the emotion of the past four years completely overwhelming her at that moment. Raffaele looked elated as the verdicts were read, and in a very telling moment, he was hugged by one of the guards. Amanda and Raffaele were given no time at all to embrace family members as both were immediately taken out of the courtroom by armed guards. This was most likely a precaution taken to assure their safety and it was wonderful to know that this was the last time that Amanda and Raffaele would be under the control of armed captors.

Several news agencies were as confused as I was by Hellmann's words, causing them to report that the appeal had failed. This error was not only embarrassing but exposed just how dishonest some news outlets are. The Daily Mail not only posted incorrect headlines, but they also went as far as to report fabricated responses, "Unreal. A nightmare. Speechless," It read: "As Knox realized the enormity of what Judge Hellmann was saying, she sank into her chair sobbing uncontrollably while her family and friends hugged each other in tears." The website even managed to find "sources" to comment on the false verdict: "Prosecutors were delighted with the verdict and said that 'justice has been done." Although they said: "on a human factor it was sad two young people would be spending years in jail."

I think it was a small victory to see the media embarrassed on the day that Amanda and Raffaele were declared innocent. It reinforced what I have been saying about the media coverage of this case for years, all while giving a little pay back to those who have caused so much damage.

The coverage coming from inside the courtroom, revealed an audience that was overwhelmingly supportive, but that could not be said for those waiting outside, as that crowd was more mixed. Amanda's sister Deanna was met with cheers when she addressed the crowd outside the courtroom, but soon after, a group assembled to protest the verdicts. Unfortunately, this group would end up fighting amongst themselves, appearing to be nothing more than a drunken mob taking advantage of the situation.

When Amanda returned to Capanne prison to collect her belongings, she was humbled to find hundreds of fellow inmates cheering from their cells chanting her name. Many inmates hung clothing out of their windows like flags in a symbolic showing of support.

In Seattle a small group of supporters held a televised all night vigil as they awaited the verdict. Unfortunately I was unable to attend, but viewing the reactions of those at the vigil that I have come to know over the past two years was a very emotional experience for me. This was a fulfilling victory for many who have worked tirelessly for a cause that they believed in.

Coming Home
On the day that Amanda was finally declared innocent and given her freedom, it was not the United States Government that helped Amanda plan her trip home, it was the Italy-USA Foundation led by Italian politician Rocco Girlanda and the foundation's secretary general

Corrado Daclon that would help to ensure Amanda's smooth exit from Italy.

There is a very emotional picture (as seen in the photo section) showing Amanda as she passed through the gates of the prison for the last time, holding the hand of Daclon. The truth is more clear than ever. This case was never about Italy vs. United States. This injustice was caused by a small group of individuals led by a rogue prosecutor. We may never know just how much support Amanda received from Italy. Hopefully someday, someone will tell the story.

When Amanda arrived home, a quick press conference was organized, giving Amanda the opportunity to thank her supporters. Media trucks were lined up, as Amanda's plane touched down in Seattle, just hoping to get a glimpse of her first steps back on American soil. Even though the local media was all over Amanda at the airport, all three major networks in Seattle did something unprecedented, promising to leave Amanda alone once she arrived home, stating that no cameras or reporters would show up at Amanda's home without the request of Amanda or her family. The local media's decision was a wonderful gesture, unfortunately other media outlets outside of Seattle would not follow suit.

The press conference took place shortly after Amanda's plane arrived at the airport, lasting only a few minutes, with Ted Simon being the first to speak:

> *"It has been a trying and grueling four year nightmarish marathon that no child or parent should have to endure. But Amanda and her parents, Curt,*

*Edda, Chris, and Cassandra, have displayed
unquestioned and unparalleled patience, steadfast
courage, dignity, resilience, and fortitude. But most of
all, they have relied upon their faith that this unjust
conviction would not stand. They have persevered
with unusual grace and under extremely difficult
circumstances."*

Simon went on to thank the court for re-examining the
evidence and having the courage to correct the errors of
the lower court, stating that the court's decision un-
mistakenly announces to the world that Amanda Knox
was wrongly convicted and that she was absolutely not
responsible for the tragic loss of Meredith Kercher.

Simon concluded by reminding everyone that
Meredith was Amanda's friend and that Amanda and her
family would like everyone to keep Meredith and her
family in their prayers. Then came an extremely
emotional moment as Amanda stood to take the podium.
With her family there to support her (just as they had
done throughout her entire ordeal), Amanda spoke
briefly, choking back her tears, thanking those who have
supported her and her family:

*"They are reminding me to speak in English. I am
having problems with that. I'm really overwhelmed
right now. I was looking down from the airplane and
it seemed like everything wasn't real. What is
important for me to say is just thank you to everyone
who has believed in me, who has defended me, who
has supported my family. My family is the most
important thing to me right now and I just want to go
be with them. So thank you for being there for me."*

Shortly after the press conference ended, several people were asking where Amanda's step father Chris Mellas was. Chris has shown amazing support for Amanda, moving to Perugia, vowing not to come home without his step daughter. So why wasn't he at the press conference? Well, we would later find out that Chris was not far away, as the limousines brought Amanda's family to their home, Chris and Amanda took off in another direction in his car, bringing Amanda to an undisclosed location so she could enjoy some privacy. The family would all reunite shortly thereafter.

When the emotional journey home was complete and things began to settle down, it became possible to take a closer look at Hellmann's decision to uphold the slander charge against Amanda. This charge was satisfied with time served, but Amanda was ordered to pay Patrick Lumumba a monetary sum. According to Frank Sfarzo, her attorneys will more than likely be able to reverse Hellmann's decision on appeal. Now that Amanda has been declared innocent, the slander charge makes no sense. The only logical reason to knowingly accuse an innocent man would be to protect yourself from prosecution. Knowing that Amanda is innocent of the crime, what could her motivation possibly have been? It is more clear than ever that Amanda was telling the truth when she described her interrogation. The information about Lumumba was obtained by means of a coerced confession during a brutal interrogation administered by members of the Perugian police department. Lumumba was right to file a lawsuit against the police but certainly not against Amanda Knox.

I believe that Hellmann's decision to confirm the charge of slander was more symbolic that anything. By upholding that one charge, Hellmann allowed all involved to save face. With the court's decision, Amanda and Raffaele gained their freedom and Mignini and company, in theory, would move on unscathed. As disappointing as this might sound, the court still deserves credit for having the courage to correct the injustice committed against Amanda and Raffaele. The key will be for the citizens of Perugia to see that Hellmann's decision does not actually absolve those responsible for the wrongful convictions. It will be up to the citizens of Perugia to stand up against the current Mignini led police-state, if they ever expect any significant reform.

Unfortunately negative news stories continue to surface about Amanda and Raffaele, and the court's decision to save face certainly motivates those who will forever believe that Amanda and Raffaele are guilty to continue to do everything in their power to keep the story alive.

It must be stressed that Judge Hellmann spoke loud and clear when he declared that Amanda Knox and Raffaele Sollecito are innocent, stating that they had absolutely nothing to do with Meredith Kercher's murder.

In the case of the murder (and the sexual assault, transporting the knife, and theft), Amanda and Raffaele were acquitted "for not having committed the act."

With regard to the charge of staging a burglary, Amanda and Raffaele were acquitted "because the act does not exist." (Hellmann's court ruled that the burglary was not staged)

Hellmann's words "because the act does not exist" said what we have been saying all along; the break in was real. Rudy Guede broke the window in order to gain entry to the cottage. There was no knife taken from Raffaele's apartment, no sex game, and no staged break in. Nothing that was suggested by Mignini and his marionettes turned out to be true. Meredith was attacked in her own home when she walked in on a burglary in progress. As so many have said all along, this was a horrible crime but not a complicated one.

Unfortunately, Hellmann's ruling will never be enough for some people. There is no doubt that irreparable damage is caused whenever someone is wrongly accused of a crime. Many will forever believe the initial accusation regardless of any information they hear in the future.

Injustice in Perugia discussed those who will forever see Amanda and Raffaele in a negative light when we coined the name "guilter" in March 2010. What exactly does guilter mean? A guilter is someone that believes in the guilt of Amanda Knox and Raffaele Sollecito regardless of any evidence that is presented proving otherwise. A guilter will continue to believe that Amanda and Raffaele are guilty long after they are acquitted. Guilters are people that bought into all of the lies that were leaked to the press from the beginning of the trial to the present. Guilters continue to spread these lies long after they have been completely refuted.

I am hopeful that all news on this case will soon fade, giving Amanda and Raffaele the chance to get a fresh start. Neither one of them asked for fame during their incarceration and certainly do not seek it now. The same goes for Amanda and Raffaele's family members, as they were all dragged into the same nightmare. Many lives were put on hold in order to support their loved ones in need. It will take time for life to resume to some kind of normal, and both families deserve privacy and respect as they move forward.

Those who have shown support for Amanda and Raffaele should be mindful that the two do not owe anything to anyone. They are not obligated to answer a single question or to pose for a single photo. No one who has supported them should ever expect anything in return for their contributions. For me, Hellmann provided all that I will ever need, when it comes to a return on my investment, when he declared Amanda and Raffaele innocent. Anyone that has actively supported Amanda and Raffaele should find great satisfaction in the outcome. We won! What else could we possibly need? Mission accomplished.

I wish Amanda and Raffaele nothing but the best and I hope they are both able to find happiness while living long fulfilling lives in peace.

After four long years, Amanda and Raffaele were able to find justice, but that does not eliminate the fact that serious reform is needed in Perugia, Italy. Hopefully this case will shine a light on the massively corrupt police force that currently holds power in Perugia, causing the Perugian population to demand swift change, so that justice will be rightfully attainable for all. For this to happen, Giuliano Mignini, Patrizia Stefanoni, Edgardo Giobbi, and others, must be prosecuted for their corruption. If those involved are not properly punished for their actions, then the door will remain wide open for history to repeat itself over and over again. Going after the big guns may seem like an impossible task, but it is well within reach if the citizens of Perugia are willing to see it through, and it is vital if Perugia ever intends to truly find justice.

Now that Amanda and Raffaele are free, there is no longer a need for Injustice in Perugia to remain active. The website will remain online for those seeking information on the case but updates will soon stop as it is time to move on. Even though our work is done with this case, it does not mark the end for our group. We will soon begin our next project, reaching out to bring more knowledge and attention to wrongful convictions all around the world. We will soon launch the website www.injustice-anywhere.org and we will start out once again to gather support for our new group "Injustice Anywhere."

Wrongful convictions occur all around the world. We must do more to prevent the unjust imprisonment of innocent people, and in doing so, we must focus on the larger picture, not just the cases we see highlighted on television. If we choose to turn our backs on this epidemic, we risk creating more victims like Clarence Elkins, Christopher Turner, and Danny Brown. Who are these people? Even though their cases were not sensational enough to get the attention of Anderson Cooper, they were all cases of wrongful conviction, only to be corrected after each had lost many years of their lives. There are hundreds of similar cases that go mostly unnoticed, but are of no less importance than any case that happens to attract the attention of the media.

Please do not turn your back on this growing problem. Please take the time to learn more about wrongful convictions and be sure to check out injustice-anywhere.org for news and updates. Together we can all make a difference.

Recommended Websites

Injustice in Perugia (www.injusticeinperugia.org)

**Injustice in Perugia Member's Forum
(www.injusticeinperugiaforum.org)**

Injustice Blog (injusticeinperugia.blogspot.com)

The injustice in Perugia websites will remain online for those who are still interested in learning more about the case.

Science Spheres (www.sciencespheres.org)

Mark Waterbury, Ph.D., has done extensive research regarding this case. His blog reviews the distorted and pseudoscientific evidence developed by the prosecution to justify their incarceration. Mark is also the author of "The Monster of Perugia – The Framing of Amanda Knox", a book about the case.

Friends of Amanda (www.friendsofamanda.org)

This site provides detailed information about this case. Jim Lovering does an excellent job of presenting information in an easy to read format with well organized links to his sources.

Raffaele Sollecito (www.raffaelesollecito.org)

This is an excellent place to learn about the real Raffaele Sollecito. The media often ignores Raffaele even though he suffered equally in this ordeal. Please visit this website and learn more about Raffaele.

The Ridiculous Case Against Amanda Knox and Raffaele Sollecito (knoxarchives.blogspot.com)

Ray Turner's blog is excellent for those interested in reading more about Giuliano Mignini's corruption charges and strong-armed tactics.

View-From-Wilmington (www.viewfromwilmington.blogspot.com)

Chris Halkides, associate professor of chemistry and biochemistry at the University of North Carolina at Wilmington, has written a series of excellent articles in regard to the case.

Let's Talk about True Crime (blog.seattlepi.com/Dempsey/index.asp)

Candace Dempsey's true crime blog offers extensive coverage on the case and continues to provide topic related updates. Candace is also the author of "Murder in Italy", a book about the case.

Innocence Project (www.innocenceproject.org)

Please visit this Website to learn more about wrongful convictions. The site is an excellent resource for up to date information. Please get involved. The innocence project has helped to free hundreds of wrongfully convicted people. They are a great organization that needs your support.

Thank you to Andrew Lowery for designing the cover for this book, and to Jim Lovering, Joseph Bishop, and the Italy–USA Foundation for providing photographs.